How To Be A

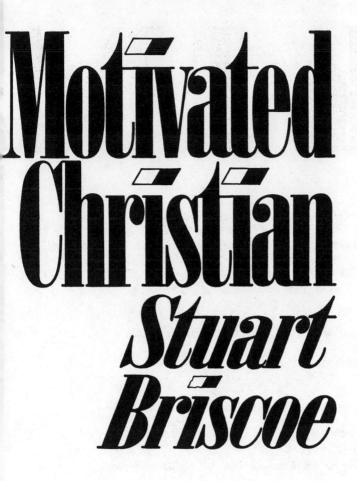

Motivated Christian

Stuart Briscoe

VICTOR BOOKS™

A DIVISION OF SCRIPTURE PRESS PUBLICATIONS INC.
USA CANADA ENGLAND

Unless otherwise indicated, Scripture quotations are from the HOLY BIBLE, NEW INTERNATIONAL VERSION, © 1973, 1978, 1984, International Bible Society. Used by permission of Zondervan Bible Publishers. Others are from the KING JAMES VERSION (KJV) and THE NEW KING JAMES VERSION (NKJV), © 1979, 1980, 1982, Thomas Nelson, Inc., Publishers.

Recommended Dewey Decimal Classification: 248.4

Suggested Subject Heading: CHRISTIAN LIVING

Library of Congress Catalog Card Number: 86-63153

ISBN: 0-89693-179-X

This special edition is published with permission from the original publisher, Scripture Press Publications, Inc., 1825 College Avenue, Wheaton, IL 60187.

VICTOR BOOKS
A division of SP Publications, Inc.
Wheaton, Illinois 60187

contents

To those who make things happen—
  may this book be an encouragement to continue.

To those who watch things happen—
  may this book be a stimulus to get involved.

To those who didn't realize anything was happening—
  may this book administer a nudge in the appropriate place.

preface

The expressions may vary—"burnout," "running out of gas," "I've had it up to here." But whatever the terminology, there seems to be a lot of Christians around who have lost (or never had) enthusiasm for life in general and serving the Lord in particular. What's the problem? I think it's a matter of motivation.

You see, when we decide to do something we concentrate on the methods, the money, the manpower, and the means—all of which are important. But without motivation channeled in the right direction, the money is wasted; the methods prove impractical; the manpower becomes disillusioned and disgruntled; and the means, instead of achieving an end, become the end itself. The dreary business of trying to keep the ship afloat is perpetuated . . . and sometimes the ship is not going anywhere.

Motivation is the key in all areas of human endeavor. But when we talk about Christian living and service (and the two cannot be separated) we have to recognize the profound significance of motivation because of the extraordinary and demanding distinctives of Christian behavior and lifestyle. Let's face it, the man in the street who subscribes to such popular maxims as, "Don't get mad—get even!"

does not need the same motivation as the Christian who has bought into the principle, "Love your enemies." The hedonist finds inner resources to motivate his self-centeredness which prove totally inadequate to the believer who sincerely wishes to operate by the Bible's command, "Whatever you do, do it heartily as unto the Lord."

But the good news is that if Christianity makes unique demands, it also offers unique motivational dynamics. What these motivational forces are and how they work is the subject of this book. They are not abstract studies either, because they are taken from the passages of Scripture in which the great Apostle Paul (a motivated man if ever there was one) took the lid off his own head and allowed believers of his day to peek into his inner workings to find out what made him tick.

So I hope this book will challenge and encourage those who profess to "serve the Lord Christ" and also introduce the unconvinced to the vitality and viability of Christianity lived in the power of the Spirit. And for anyone who reads these pages whose "get up and go has got up and went," I hope this book will prod him or her into a new surge of delight in living uniquely and winsomely for the Lord Jesus.

Because I am fortunate enough to pastor a large church, I am surrounded by hundreds of wonderful believers whose motivation serves to encourage and support me. Many of them have had a part in the birth and growth of this book. They sat quietly through the sermons in which these concepts first saw the light of day. Many of them worked hard in our tape ministry to make the messages available on a wider basis. A team of them sat down endlessly and transcribed the tapes (you try transcribing a forty-five-minute talk and see how long it takes!); others edited tapes for radio; another team helped produce TV shows and video cassettes of the same material. While I preached motivation they got on with it! Happy the preacher who ministers in such a situation. Special mention must go to Pam Kennedy, the wife of a naval officer, who, while he is at sea, spends her time caring for her family and using her considerable literary and editorial skills helping preachers like me put the spoken word in written form. To all these people, my family, and my friends, I express my gratitude.

"Now, brothers, I want to remind you of the Gospel
I preached to you, which you received and on which
you have taken your stand. By this Gospel you are
saved, if you hold firmly to the word I have preached
to you. Otherwise, you have believed in vain.

"For what I received I passed on to you as of first
importance: that Christ died for our sins according to
the Scriptures, that He was buried, that He was
raised on the third day according to the Scriptures,
and that He appeared to Peter, and then to the
Twelve. After that, He appeared to more than five
hundred of the brothers at the same time, most of
whom are still living, though some have fallen asleep.
Then He appeared to James, then to all the apostles,
and last of all He appeared to me also, as to one abnormally born.

"For I am the least of the apostles and do not
even deserve to be called an apostle, because I persecuted the church of God. But by the grace of God I
am what I am, and His grace to me was not without
effect. No, I worked harder than all of them—yet
not I, but the grace of God that was with me."

1 CORINTHIANS 15:1-10

one
THE GRATITUDE ATTITUDE

All of us have watched the Olympics on TV and have no doubt been tremendously moved by the performances of so many of the world's top amateur athletes.

When we see U.S. track star Carl Lewis place first in the long jump and win the hundred meters in 9.9 seconds we might be tempted to say, "Wow, it doesn't take long to win a gold medal, does it? Just one jump, or a 9.9 second run!" But, of course, we know better than that. We know that a tremendous amount of training has gone into winning those gold medals. We also recognize the fact that many of the people who did so well in the Olympics were people who were highly motivated. Some had overcome serious physical handicaps; others, severe financial problems; still others, great emotional stress, and yet they had been somehow able to persevere. And I don't suppose any of us will forget, in the 1984 games, the sight of the Swiss girl at the end of the women's marathon, totally out of it with heat exhaustion, yet motivated to keep going.

Motivation is a phenomenally important subject, particularly as far as believers in Jesus Christ are concerned. What is it that motivates the believer to live differently? What motivates a believer to put up with persecution? What motivates a believer to keep on keeping on when society around him tends to be going in the opposite direction? What motivates a believer to be sacrificial when everything within him screams to be selfish? There has to be a powerful motivating factor here, and we need to know what it is and be able to explore it.

THE GRACE OF GOD: A DIVINE ATTITUDE

The Apostle Paul gives us a very helpful insight into Christian motivation in 1 Corinthians 15 where he speaks on three occasions in verse 10 about the grace of God. We notice first of all that he says, "By the grace of God I am what I am." Then secondly, he adds that God's grace was not without effect. "I worked harder than all of them." And then thirdly, he says that it was "not I, but the grace of God that was with me."

The first time that Paul mentions the grace of God, he's talking about the divine attitude. As he puts it, "I am what I am because of God's grace." The second time he mentions the grace of God, it's as a dynamic stimulus. He says in effect, "The grace of God operates within me so much that I work harder than all of the other people." He is motivated, he is stimulated by the grace of God. But then Paul quickly does an evangelical sidestep when he realizes that having said he worked harder than all the others, some of the apostles might have their apostolic noses bent out of shape. So he adds, "It was not I, but the grace of God who worked alongside." It is God's grace operative on a daily basis which enables him to be what he is.

The grace of God is a divine attitude. The grace of God is a dynamic stimulus. The grace of God is a daily enabling. These three statements are the focus of this chapter.

Now, if we want to understand what Paul means by the grace of God, we have to explore his words, "By the grace of God I am what I am." From that process comes the obvious question, "What are you, Paul?" Two answers are found in this passage of Scripture. First of all, he calls himself an apostle, albeit the least of the apostles. He stresses his apostleship in his letters to the Corinthians, because apostleship is a position of privilege, a position of authority, and a position of responsibility. And so, he doesn't back off at all. He says, "I am an apostle." But then immediately, he adds something else very strange. He says that when Christ appeared to him, He appeared to "one abnormally born" (verse 8), or as another translation has it, "one born out of due time" (KJV). But no matter what Bible version, all of them have one thing in common; they carefully avoid saying what Paul actually said. The reason being that what he said was rather coarse and crude, and the translators apparently feel that we're not up to that kind of coarseness and crudity. Evidently, the translators haven't been listening to the way people talk nowadays.

The word that Paul uses here translated "born out of due time" or "abnormally born" is the word that literally means "the product of an abortion or miscarriage." Therefore, what he says is this: "Christ appeared to me, one like the product of an abortion or the result of a miscarriage." Now that's gross! You don't talk about that in polite company unless, of course, you're an apostle. And, of course, if you're a preacher, you can quote the apostle! The contrast is hard to miss. On the one hand, the Apostle Paul calls himself an apostle; on the other hand, he calls himself an abortion.

One of the things I learned when I first came to the United States from Britain was the American penchant for putting everything in its proper slot and giving it its proper name. For example, I discovered that people have self-images. I suppose the British have them; they just don't know that's what you call them! When I began to learn about self-images from Americans, I found out that there are high self-images as well as low self-images; then I became curious about the self-images of Bible characters.

For instance, does Paul have a high self-image or a low self-image? The answer is obvious. He has a high self-image.

He says, "I am an apostle. I have authority. You guys in Corinth had better shape up. I have a word from the Lord." But then we run into a problem, because immediately he adds, "I am like the product of an abortion." Now I've met people with low self-images but none quite that low, and so I asked myself, "Does Paul have a high self-image or a low self-image, or is he perhaps schizophrenic?"

The answer is that he views himself two different ways. If he looks at himself as he is without God, he sees a person singularly unsatisfactory and singularly unpleasant—the product of an abortion. On the other hand, if he looks at himself as God has taught him to look at himself, he sees an apostle. Somehow he is able to live in the tension of the two. He sees himself as he is in himself, but then he sees himself as God sees him and as God has called him to function. Therefore, he is able to say, "It is by the grace of God that I, an abortion, am an apostle." If we are to understand the grace of God in Paul's case, we must see that Paul's understanding of the grace of God is this: God has chosen, of all things, abortions to become apostles.

Now then, if we try to apply Paul's understanding to ourselves, we must ask how many of us have such low self-images we think of ourselves as being like the products of abortions? Probably very few. On the other hand, how many of us feel that we are apostles? Again, probably very few. But if we ask how many of us fit in between, most of us would answer yes. And here's the point. The thing that really helps me understand the grace of God is to understand how close to an abortion I am, and how near to an apostle I've become.

All of us need to live in that tension. We need to sense how near to abortions we are, and how close to apostles we have become. Let's amplify that.

First of all, the Bible clearly teaches that we're all moral failures (Romans 3:10, 23; Psalm 143:2, et al.). In the same way that George Orwell wrote in his classic *Animal Farm*, that all pigs are equal but some are more equal than others, there is no question that some of us have failed more than others. Nonetheless, God says we *all* have come short of His glory.

Secondly, if we accept the biblical truth that all of us have lived unsatisfactorily before God, we must also recognize the biblical truth that God is absolutely just and right, holy and true. In other words, He is the antithesis of all that He finds fault with in us. And because of His character, He has to deal with moral failures justly and rightly. He has to give us exactly what we deserve—His condemnation.

Thirdly, we must recognize that there's nothing we can do about our moral failure and absolutely nothing we can do about God's justice. As far as Stuart Briscoe's moral failure is concerned, I may *feel* I can turn over a new leaf and do better, and it's possible I may indeed *turn* over a new leaf and *do* better, but that does not erase the fifty-six years I've lived so far. I cannot suddenly go back in time and do all the things I ought to have done and didn't. I cannot backtrack fifty-six years and redo all the things that I did and shouldn't have done. In a sense, I am morally incapable of changing what I am or what I've done. So perhaps I entertain a sneaking, lingering hope that I can change God. Maybe in *my* case He won't be just, He won't be righteous, maybe somehow or other *I'll* get off scot-free. But in the same way that I cannot change my own moral failure, there is no way that I can tinker with the justice and the righteousness of God. If that is true, then it leads me to an appalling conclusion: I have to accept the fact that God is free to deal with me as He chooses.

Now, that is one of the most astounding conclusions that a human being can ever reach, and it is one that our society resists and resents. There's no shortage of people who talk "God talk." There's no shortage of people who quite happily go to church. There's no shortage of people who talk quite warmly about Jesus. There is, however, a marked shortage of people who will admit, "I, a moral failure in the eyes of the holy God, am incapable of altering my failed state."

Why? Because it is the most humbling thing a human being can say, and human beings aren't known for their humility.

If it is true that God is free to deal with us as He chooses, the most important question we can ask is, "What has God chosen?" The answer: He has decided to mingle mercy and grace with His justice. Now, what does that mean? *Justice* means we get what we deserve; *mercy* means we don't get all we deserve; *grace* gives us what we don't deserve. And God has figured out how to deal with us on the basis of all three at the same time.

Let me illustrate this, because initially it sounds quite complicated. Picture a father confronting his small son because of the boy's unsatisfactory behavior. He tells his son that he has been disobedient, that wrong actions have consequences, and that he's going to have to be punished.

Then he adds, "Son, this is going to hurt me more than it's going to hurt you."

To which his son replies, "Well, I don't want you to hurt yourself, Dad."

Undaunted, the father continues, "I am going to administer justice to you. I'm going to apply this board of education ten times to the seat of your learning."

This is justice. The child is getting what he deserves.

After eight, the father stops and says, "OK, Son, that will do."

The son says, "You said ten, Dad. You only gave me eight; you haven't done justice."

The father replies, "Yes, I've mingled justice with mercy. I gave you what you deserved, but I didn't give you all you deserved. Now, go to your room; I want you to think about what you did, about what I've said, about what happened, and then come to some conclusions. All right, Son?"

"All right."

Half an hour later, Dad calls upstairs and says, "I'm going for ice cream; would you like to come with me, Son?"

And the son says, "Why would I want to come and watch you eat ice cream?"

And the father says, "No, I'm going to buy *you* the ice cream—three scoops, all the sticky goop on top of it, even nuts and cherries."

And the son says, "Who's paying, Dad?"

And Dad says, "I am."

With that, the son comes running downstairs and says, "Why, Dad, why?"

And Dad simply says, "It's called grace, Son. It's called grace."

Justice gives the boy what he deserves; mercy doesn't give him all he deserves; grace gives him what he doesn't deserve. Similarly, God freely chooses to deal with humanity by mingling justice with mercy and grace.

How does it work? The expression in Scripture is "in Christ." The wages of sin is death, writes Paul to the Romans. If I'm to be given what I deserve, then I have to recognize that death is the payment for sin. Thankfully, God devised a way whereby He could justly give me what I deserve, but, mercifully, give it to me in such a way that it wouldn't destroy me. He put me "in Christ" in His economy, and when Christ died on the cross, according to the Apostle Paul, I was crucified with Him. I died with Him. I was buried with Him. But then God says that He raised me up into newness of life with Christ. He made me a child of God. He gave me eternal life. He offered me a place in heaven. He gave me the Holy Spirit. Then He committed to me a ministry and gave me the privilege of living now for His glory. But that's not all. He also promised me an eternity during which I would simply exist to the praise of His glory.

This choice of God to impart grace and mercy to me was not the result of a conference that He had with the best brains in the world; it is not the product of human ingenuity; it is not the response to some erudite suggestion from a very bright theological professor. No, this divine plan was locked up in the heart and intention of God from the very beginning.

It is God's sovereign choice to deal with me in Christ in

such a way that my sins have been judged in Christ without destroying me. I've been raised into newness of life. I have the privilege of living for His glory, being in eternity, enjoying His fatherhood, living like His Son, and doing something of eternal significance. And it's all because of grace. It is the divine attitude.

THE GRACE OF GOD: A DYNAMIC STIMULUS

Now, let's get back to Paul. Realizing all God had done on his behalf, the Apostle Paul got the message, and he said, "I can't believe it. Me, of all people, being invited by God to live in this kind of an experience. Not because of who I am, not because of what I've done, but solely because of who God is in Christ. He redeemed me by His grace."

And when we start thinking like that, we'll begin to get a handle on a fundamental Christian doctrine, the doctrine of the grace of God.

How does this affect us? Well, it can leave us bored out of our skulls. We can say, "Who cares about all this theology stuff? Does God really understand the kind of world we're living in? Does He want us stuck in some Christian ivory tower debating justice and mercy and grace?" No, and neither did Paul. Understanding the grace of God is not, to him, understanding cold theological dogma. Understanding the grace of God is to be ignited by the most powerful motivating factor in the world, for the Apostle Paul says the grace of God was not wasted on him. Indeed, he worked harder than all of them because the grace of God was operative in his life.

My schooling was in the British educational system. One of the nice things about that is that they require students to take English language, English literature, Latin, and another modern language—at least they did in those days. So I spent a lot of time studying languages. I took six years of Latin and didn't do very well, but there are some things that I remember. One of them is this: the word for *grace* in Latin is *gratia*, from which the word *gratitude* also has its roots. That's the key here. *Gratia* or grace is the root from which gratitude grows. What is this powerful Christian motivation of which Paul speaks? It is this: to understand the *gratia* of God, and then to be ignited by a tremendous sense of gratitude.

All kinds of things can motivate us, but most of them will do so for only a short time and then wear off. But the thing that will *consistently* motivate us is to make certain that we grasp the overwhelming sense that we are what we are by the grace of God. When that grasps us and we grasp it, then we will discover that *gratia* produces gratitude.

Have you noticed how hard it is to motivate people? Have you ever noticed how *you* try to do it? You challenge them, plead with them, threaten them, perhaps even bribe them, and then you discover that whatever you do, it eventually wears a bit thin. Not so with the gratitude attitude that spills from understanding God's grace.

The gratitude attitude is doing things as unto the Lord because we have a handle on *gratia*. When we get into a ministry, we may be overlooked. We may be misunderstood. We may be misquoted. Everything we do may backfire. We may become terribly discouraged and tempted to quit. That's understandable—unless we have an inner motivating power that has absolutely nothing to do with the reactions of people around us. If we're praised, fine. If we're ignored, fine. If they understand us, fine. If they misunderstand us, fine. If they rightly represent us, fine. If they misrepresent us, fine. What really matters is this: out of gratitude to the Lord, we do everything as unto Him. The gratitude attitude. I'm firmly convinced that the great need in the contemporary church is for people to so grasp the grace of God that they find fire kindled within their bones. It's the gratitude attitude burning constantly within them.

Let's return to Paul's story again.

"Paul," God says, "I want to deal with you in grace."

Paul is overwhelmed. He's so thrilled, he says, "I feel a

strange sensation within me. What do You call it, Lord?"

And the Lord says, "It's called gratitude."

"How can I express my gratitude?" asks the apostle, long before André Crouch ever wrote his song on the subject.

The Lord replies, "By doing heartily what I've told you to do."

It's at this point we need to be careful. Sometimes out of gratitude we decide we're going to do all kinds of dramatic, expansive, expensive things, and we tell God so. I'm sure that the Apostle Paul probably had a few such ideas in mind when he asked the Lord, "What do You want me to do?"

"I want you to be an apostle."

"Oh, good. To the Jews?"

"No, I have an apostle to the Jews, Paul."

"You do?"

"Yes, I do."

"Who?"

"Peter."

"Peter who?"

"Peter Simon or Simon Peter."

"Ha, ha, Simon Peter, Lord. Fisherman. Not particularly gifted. In fact, only gifted in two areas. Every time he opens his mouth he puts both feet in it. Whenever he says he'll do anything, he falls asleep. Put him in prison, he falls asleep. Having his quiet time on the rooftop, he falls asleep. Take him to the Garden of Gethsemane to pray, he falls asleep. He's a very gifted foot-in-mouth operator, and he's a very, very gifted sleeper. And he is going to be the apostle to the Jews?"

"Right."

"What do You want *me* to be?"

"I would like you to be apostle to the Gentiles."

Now the true-blue Jew, Paul, gags on that one. We've got to understand how utterly unacceptable this was to him. But what happens subsequently? He becomes the superlative apostle to the Gentiles. He remains constant and consistent, to the point of exhaustion. He continues giving and giving and giving of himself to Gentiles who beat him up, throw him in jail, and eventually take his life. Why? Because the Gentiles are so great? No. Because he had such a tremendous love for Gentiles? No. Because he thought Gentiles were worthy? No. Because the Gentiles loved him? No. Why on earth did he do it then? The gratitude attitude. The gratitude attitude kept on and kept on. If you know people who've got the fire in their bones, it's the same gratitude attitude. You can see them going on, faint, yet pursuing. They keep going, because they're doing it as unto Jesus Christ.

THE GRACE OF GOD: A DAILY ENABLING

Now reflect for a moment. Do you understand the grace of God? Do you have a handle on it? Does it have a grip on you? Do you know that the thing that keeps you going is the gratitude attitude? If so, fine. There can be a problem in all this, however. Although out of gratitude you may feel God is calling you to do many things, you also may feel that you're running out of gas. The Apostle Paul has a word for all of us on this subject as well. He continues to point out that it is not he who is doing the work, but the grace of God that works alongside.

In the same way that the Latin word *gratia* helped us to understand God's grace earlier, so the Greek word will help us here. The Greek word for grace is *charis*. It is the word from which we get *charisma*. We don't know what charisma is, but we know if people have it. To a very large extent, we are now finding that elections are governed by how much charisma a person can project on the television screen. We read books like *The Marketing of the President* and begin to discover how we live in an image-oriented, not a concept-oriented society. If we can produce and project an image that has charisma, whatever it is, then we're successful.

What is charisma? Well, it's a certain indefinable gift. It's something that you've got because you're given it, *graced* with it. Grace has a habit of gifting people. A *charismatic* Christian is one who is particularly interested in spiritual gifts.

Now, where does this leave us? It leaves us at the point of recognizing that God in His grace daily gifts us. Of course, the superlative gift that He has given us is the Holy Spirit, but even more beautiful is the fact that when the gift of the Holy Spirit is granted to us, He brings His own gifts. So we are doubly gifted. We are first gifted with the presence of the Holy Spirit; then we are gifted by the Holy Spirit with specific gifts that enable us to do what God wants us to do.

God doesn't tell Paul to be the apostle to the Gentiles without first giving him the Holy Spirit. Neither does He tell Paul to be a great writer of theology without giving him a mind that can grapple with theology. God says to Paul, "I will give you the power and the gifts to be what I want you to be and to do what I want you to do. What is more, I'll keep them coming every single day. Every single day, I will go on enabling you." That's how the grace of God works.

Some time ago, at the end of the third Sunday worship service, I was ready to head out the door. I preach a great appetite on Sunday, and I was ready to go home and have my dinner. But somebody told me, much to my chagrin, that a reporter from one of the Milwaukee newspapers wanted to talk to me. He'd been at the church all morning, walking around, taking pictures, and now he wanted an interview. Finally, he pushed through the folks at the end of the third service, and confronted me. He didn't introduce himself, didn't say hello, didn't say it was an interview.

He barked, "Would you say you're gifted?"

I answered, "Yes."

He said, "I think you're arrogant."

I said, "Well, I think you're ignorant." But quickly I added, "Time out. That wasn't a very good start, was it?"

I continued, "Perhaps I should explain what's going on here. The reason you think I'm arrogant is that when you asked me if I was gifted, I said yes. Now, the reason you're ignorant is this: you wouldn't have asked that question if you had known something very simple and very basic about Christianity. There is no such thing as an ungifted Christian. Every Christian has the gift of the Holy Spirit, and every person who has the Holy Spirit has the gifts of the Holy Spirit or at least some gift of the Spirit. Therefore, your question was based on not knowing and asked out of ignorance. But I've got great news for you, and it is this: you now know the facts, so you're no longer ignorant. I may still be arrogant, but you're no longer ignorant." (I'd rather be an arrogant truth-teller than a humble liar, especially about the Holy Spirit.) The truth is that every believer is gifted—or "graced."

The electricity in our church building is a superlative energy source. Innumerable appliances can be plugged into the system. Plug in the microphone and it amplifies my voice. Plug in the lights and they brighten the whole auditorium. Plug in the organ and it is ready to provide beautiful music. Plug in the TV cameras and they pick up images. Turn on the air conditioning and the church cools off. Plug in the heating and it warms up. Same power, different appliances.

Every believer you've ever met, every believer you'll ever meet, has received the gift of the Holy Spirit. And the Holy Spirit is the electricity of God. Every believer has also been given his own special appliances to plug into the power source so that God might make him an air conditioner or an amplifier. He might make him burst out with organ music, or he might project an image on a screen. Whatever it is that he's called to be, God daily gifts him for it, for no other reason than He has freely chosen to. It's called grace.

The church of Jesus Christ is a group of people in touch with the grace of God, on fire because of the grace of God, with the burning motivation of the gratitude attitude.

Every one of them is empowered by the Holy Spirit. Every one of them is gifted by the Holy Spirit. Why? So that they might be what He called them to be—enthusiastically and thoroughly—as an expression of gratitude. No wonder the church of Jesus Christ can be and should be the most phenomenally dynamic community wherever people live. Why isn't it, so often? I believe one reason is this: too often we try to motivate people the wrong way. The only way truly successful Christians can consistently be motivated is to be constantly in touch with what it means to be a recipient of the grace of God.

Let's take a little self-examination. Do you really know the grace of God in your life? Is your life motivated by that grace? Are you able to sense, on a daily basis, God's empowering and His enabling? Do you set out, day after day, to be to the glory of God what He has called you to be? If so, you're motivated by Christ. You're influenced by the gratitude attitude.

PERSONAL REFLECTION

Take a quiet moment to think about these things. Perhaps you have not really understood God's grace before and you'd like to respond to it. You might pray these or other similar words: "Dear Lord, I recognize that there's so much wrong with my life in Your eyes, and I recognize that You must deal with me justly and righteously, which means that I can expect Your disapproval. But I thank You that You have freely chosen to offer me forgiveness in Christ. This is a beautiful thing.

"I also understand that there is no free lunch. You offer me freely what Christ paid for with His life. It cost me nothing. It cost Christ everything. I thank You for His death which counts as my death, the wages of sin. I thank You for His resurrection, which allows me to come into newness of life. I thank You for the presence of the Holy Spirit, whom You offer to all those who truly believe, and I ask You now, please, for Christ's sake, to forgive me, to reconcile me to Yourself, to impart to me Your Spirit, that I might live a new life, not motivated by selfishness or greed or fear or reward, but motivated simply and humbly by gratitude."

Perhaps you have been a believer for some time but have forgotten the truths that first brought you to Christ. Your prayer might be as follows: "Gracious Lord, thank You for reminding me of grace. Thank You that I sense within me, even now, a welling up of gratitude. Help me to identify what You want me to do, then enable me by Your Spirit to do it in such a way that my life will be a constant hymn of praise, a sacrificial offering, a bringing of myself on a daily basis, just simply saying, 'Thank You.' What a difference this will make to my attitude, my family, my ministry, my life. Hear my prayer, dear Lord. I present it in the name of our Lord Jesus."

"Though I am free and belong to no man, I make myself a slave to everyone, to win as many as possible. To the Jews I became like a Jew, to win the Jews. To those under the Law I became like one under the Law (though I myself am not under the Law), so as to win those under the Law. To those not having the Law I became like one not having the Law (though I am not free from God's law but am under Christ's law), so as to win those not having the Law. To the weak I became weak, to win the weak. I have become all things to all men so that by all possible means I might save some. I do all this for the sake of the Gospel, that I might share in its blessings."

1 CORINTHIANS 9:19-23

two
THE SERVANT SPIRIT

A man came out of his club one evening and walked to the parking lot toward his brand-new, sparkling Cadillac. As he approached, he saw a shadowy figure bending over it, and so he grabbed hold from behind, assuming the person was damaging his car. To his surprise, it was a young boy of about eleven, who said, "Sir, I wasn't hurting your car; I was studying it."

The man said, "If you were studying it, what make is it?"

"It's a Cadillac," answered the lad.

"What year is it?"

" '84."

"What color?"

"Maroon."

And then the boy went on to recite all the minute details of the car, making it perfectly obvious to the man that he was telling the truth. The two got into a conversation about the car, and in the end the young fellow asked, "Sir, how much did this car cost you?"

"It didn't cost me anything," the man replied. "I didn't buy it."

"You stole it?" the boy asked.

"No," said the man, "I didn't steal it. My brother gave it to me."

And the boy blurted out, "Oh, I wish..."

And the man said, "I'll finish the line for you. You were going to say, 'I wish I had a brother like that.' "

And the boy replied, "No, I wasn't going to say that, sir. What I was going to say was, 'I wish I could be a brother like that.' "

The boy went on to explain that he had a sick brother at home. His parents couldn't look after him, and even at his tender age, this child had a great desire to serve his brother.

THE DEVELOPMENT OF A SERVANT SPIRIT

The attitude demonstrated by the boy in the illustration could be called the servant spirit. It is an attitude that is to be demonstrated by believers at all times, for Jesus said on one occasion to the Twelve, "The Son of man did not come to be served, but to serve" (Matthew 20:28). And it is very clear that this is the attitude He wanted to see develop in His disciples.

Now, the word *develop* is key here. The attitude of desiring to serve as opposed to wanting to be served does not come naturally. Nor does the desire to give come naturally as opposed to our inborn desire to get. There's something about us that wants to get, not give. There's something about us that wants to be served, not to serve. And yet if we're going to think in terms of Christian motivation, we've got to reckon with the fact that Christians should be characterized by the attitude of their Lord. And His attitude was: "I did not come to be served; I came to serve."

Let's look for a moment at Acts 13:36 where the Apostle Paul, speaking of King David, said these words: "When David had served God's purpose in his own generation, he fell asleep." When we think of all that David was and all that he did, we can imagine all kinds of active words to describe him. But Paul chose *served*. The reason was that David had discovered something the Apostle Paul also discovered. It is something our Lord Jesus taught and emulated: *in God's economy, you don't become great by lording it over people, but by developing the servant spirit.* David learned to serve. The Apostle Paul applauds King David for this attitude because he himself understood the significance of servanthood, as he clearly demonstrated in many of his epistles. When Paul wrote to the Thessalonians, for instance, he complimented them as a model church. Then he described their secret: "You turned to God from idols to serve the living and true God, and to wait for His Son from heaven" (1 Thessalonians 1:9-10).

To *turn to God* is a lovely expression that describes the essence of spiritual experience. There's something about us that naturally turns away from God. There's something about us that wants our own way rather than God's way. But to become a Christian there has to come a time in our lives when we turn to Him. When that turning takes place, we become open about ourselves and we demonstrate our desire to have a relationship with Him. Then we begin to draw from Him what He offers, and we move constantly closer to Him.

When we turn to God, certain things happen. First, we turn from idols. We cannot serve God and that which is opposed to God. When we come to God, we must come in submission, which means we reject that which is counter to Him. We can't have our God and our idols. If we face north, we do not have the privilege of facing south.

However, the reality of turning to God is seen in whether we are prepared not only to turn to Him, but to *serve Him as well.* And here we have a problem. Many people come to the Lord out of deep distress. Their lives are in a terrible mess; they've tried everything else to sort them out; and as a last resort they turn to God because they've been told that He will meet their needs (which is absolutely true). But if they're not careful, they may begin to picture God as nothing more than the "Need-meeter" in the sky. Projecting that further, very quickly they begin to have a relationship with God where He serves *them*, which is exactly the opposite of what it should be. God does not exist to serve us. We exist to serve Him.

The problem then becomes: how can we address the Gospel to people in deep need, convey the beauty of God's provision for that need, but at the same time bring them to the point of wanting to serve Him? The only solution I know is to concentrate on who God is, rather than on what man is. If we can concentrate on God in all His majesty and wonder, if we can show needy people how to come to Him in glad submission with an overwhelming desire to honor Him, then we can tell them, "Your hearts are now right for God to meet your needs." But if people simply come on the basis of, "God meets my needs and makes no demands," then their spiritual experience is highly questionable.

How do we acquire the correct servant attitude? In Colossians 3:23-24, Paul gives us this marvelous rule: "Whatever you do, do it heartily, as to the Lord . . . for you serve the Lord Christ" (NKJV). When we serve the living God, it doesn't mean that we have to quit our secular professions and go into "spiritual service" or even into "full-time Christian work." What we need to remember and teach others is this: whatever your occupation, as long as it is compatible with God's holiness, there is an opportunity for you, by your very demeanor, by your very commitment, by your faithfulness, by your energy, and by the expenditure of your skills, to serve the living God in that situation. You get up in the morning and thank God for a brand-new day, given from His hand, freshly baked, smelling delightful, absolutely unspoiled. You take it from Him, break it before Him as an offering, and at the end of the day, you say, "Lord, this is what I did today. I trust it brought You delight; I trust it brought You honor; I served the living God in my situation this day." Is that what you're doing? If so, you've grasped the servant spirit.

The concept of Christian service is brought into even

sharper focus when the Apostle Paul goes on to show not only that we serve the living God, but also that we serve the Christian community. Writing to the Galatians, who were struggling with the tension between legalism and licentiousness, he provides a formula.

Let me just in parentheses say what I mean here. When we travel on the Christian journey, it's a bit like steering a car. We sometimes tend to drift to the left and come precariously close to the ditch. So we swerve away from it and finish up in the ditch on the other side of the road. There's always a tendency among believers to licentious, liberal behavior. By that I mean undisciplined behavior. We say, "We're free in Christ—don't try to lay anything on us." Anything goes. Or we swerve away from that and build all kinds of restrictions, and we finish up with legalism. We've got to steer clear of both ditches. But how?

Paul's formula is this: "Do not use liberty as an opportunity for the flesh, but through love serve one another" (Galatians 5:13, NKJV). The best way to handle our liberty is not to legalistically restrict it. The best way to avoid legalism is to insist on freedom, but then to take that freedom and gladly put it into a servant mode.

One day while talking to a gentleman from my congregation he suddenly said to me, "I really am obnoxious, you know."

And I said, "Yes, you really are."

He was a little startled, I think, and continued, "I really give you a lot of abuse."

"Yes, I've noticed."

"You don't have to put up with this, you know."

"I know."

"Well, why do you?"

And I said, "Well, not because I'm the pastor, and not because you put your buck in the plate, and not because I am masochistic, but because I choose to. I'm a free agent before God, and I have made a decision and it is this: obnoxious as you are, I have chosen to serve you. I don't have to; I have freely chosen to."

That was the turning point in our relationship, and it exemplifies something very simple: in the Christian community, we make some choices. Having chosen to serve the living God, we now choose to serve our brothers and sisters in the community of believers. We don't have to. It is simply that we take our liberty and choose to exercise it lovingly by serving one another. Think of the possibilities if a congregation were comprised entirely of people who have this servant attitude: "Here I am, God, ready to serve You today. Here I am, God, identified with this particular Christian community. What can I do to serve You by serving my brothers and sisters in the community?" Each member would come in, all bright-eyed and bushy-tailed, eagerly looking for opportunities to serve. That is the servant spirit.

I was in the supermarket one day, and a lady came down the aisle whom I could barely see over the top of her groceries. I got somewhat frightened because she seemed to be heading straight for me. She screeched to a halt within a few feet of me, peered over her load, wagged her finger, and said, "I left your church. I left your church."

So I said, "Well, if it's my church, I think that was a very wise decision. If it's my church, I think I'm going to leave too."

She said, "Don't you want to know why I left?"

I said, "No, not particularly, but I think I'm going to find out." And I was right.

She said, "You weren't meeting my needs."

I answered, "I don't ever recollect seeing you before, let alone talking to you, let alone knowing your needs. Did you ever tell anyone specifically what your needs were?"

She couldn't recall that she had, so I raised another question. "Can you tell me, if we have 5,000 people sitting in that church, all with your attitude, how anyone's needs are going to be met? If you reserve the right to have that attitude, then you must give everybody the freedom to have that attitude. And if everybody has that attitude, who on earth is going to do all the need-meeting?"

Standing her ground, she demanded, "Then you tell me who will."

Relieved, I said, "I thought you'd never ask. This is what will work: when people stop sitting in the pew saying, 'They're not meeting my needs' and start saying, 'Whose needs can I meet?' Then needs will be met. When the servant spirit flourishes in a congregation, then they minister to each other as unto the Lord."

Is this what you see in the Christian community with which you identify? Are *you* one of those serving that Christian community? In exactly the same way that we, like the man with the Cadillac, would like a supergenerous brother, we would like a God who would serve us and a church that would meet our needs. But in fact, like the young boy, what we need to develop is the attitude that says, "I wish I could be a brother like that. I'd love to serve the living God and would feel so privileged to serve the Christian community."

Each of us needs to identify ways in which we're serving the living God. We need to identify the ways in which we are serving the Christian community. For this is our calling. The Apostle Paul spoke of going to areas where people had not heard of Jesus Christ, and he talked about the people who went with him and called them his fellow servants. Now that meant that he too was serving—they were serving together. What were they serving? They were serving a needy world.

We all want the world, in some way, to serve us. Many of us feel that society in general and the government in particular owe us something, when in actuality we owe our loving service to the world in the name of Christ. That's the Christian attitude, the servant spirit. We begin to develop it when we understand that servanthood is what we're called to. It's one thing to be called; it's another thing to choose to respond to what we're called to do. Millions of people in the world flock to God on the basis of Him meeting their needs, but the numbers thin out very, very quickly when they really understand that the only way to come to God is with a desire to submit to Him and to serve Him. And that is the essence of the Christian Gospel.

The choice, of course, needs to be made first of all when we recognize what a privilege it is to belong to God. It needs to be made when we recognize what a responsibility it is to be called a Christian. Our privilege and responsibility are the same as Paul's. He said, "God whose I am and whom I serve" (Acts 27:23). And he said it on the deck of a sinking ship in the middle of a storm on the Mediterranean. From an earthly perspective, everything seemed washed up for Paul, but he kept his eyes on the heavenly perspective and remembered that he belonged to God. He still couldn't help thinking in terms of serving Him. That was his privilege and that was his responsibility.

Of course, inner influences will seek to hinder us. Our own arrogance militates against wanting to serve. We prefer to be "number one," to have things revolve around us. And our own apathy often militates against serving. We just aren't interested in developing a servant spirit. Quite frankly, we are basically, fundamentally interested in what is going to be tangibly and materially to our advantage. But the servant spirit comes when, identifying with the Lord Jesus, we make certain choices and respond to what we're called to do.

Have you done that? Has the servant spirit been born within you? Is it beginning to flower and flame in your heart? That's what it means to be a spiritual person.

THE CHANNELING OF A SERVANT SPIRIT

But now let's go back to our text in Acts about David serving God's purpose. We can't just think in terms of developing a servant spirit; we have to think about ways of channeling it. When the snow begins to melt and the rain begins to fall, then the floods come and great damage ensues. But if someone comes along and spends some money, channels the flood waters, and directs them into an area where a dam can be built; if environmentalists stock the lake with fish and create a park; then the price of property around the lake escalates and a hydroelectric plant can be constructed. All that potential for disaster becomes tremendously helpful, all because the water was not left to its own devices, but was channeled. When thinking in terms of the servant spirit, let's remember this truth.

This is what Paul said. "When David had served *God's purpose*" (italics added). We channel our servant spirit first of all into an intelligent understanding of God's purpose. It's great news to know that God has a purpose for our world. It is not out of control. It is not in man's control. It is in God's hands. Scripture tells us that the same hands that brought it into being are always saving it for judgment. God is on the throne. And He tells us His plan: Jesus will be acknowledged as Lord of all. Every knee will bow to Him. Every tongue will confess Him as Lord. When that happens, God the Father will be recognized on the cosmic scale to be all in all. That's where we're heading. That's the view of the future that Scripture gives us.

But God has a *personal* plan for our lives too. To put it very simply, as the old hymn does, "There's a work for Jesus that only you can do." We need to be intelligently aware of this. Paul says, "Do not be foolish, but understand what the Lord's will is" (Ephesians 5:17). Elsewhere he exhorts believers to be "filled with the knowledge of His will" (Colossians 1:9). Yet if you talk to many Christians about knowing God's will, they often become desperately vague, terribly humble, and entirely reluctant to talk about it.

"Tell me about God's plan in your life."

They stammer, "Well, ahh. I really don't know what to say."

To them, God's will is a total mystery, and when all's said and done, far more is said than done!

I frequently talk to young people about their careers. I love it when they discuss with me their futures and all the variables. And I'm intrigued about the things they evaluate. Generally atop the list of priorities is money. Second is where they're going to live. Third is the climate. Fourth, the things they can buy with the money. Fifth is the lifestyle that they've already adopted and chosen.

I usually ask these young men and women, "Have you factored in the very real possibility that God may want you in the ministry? Have you factored in the very high possibility that God may want you in foreign missions?" More often than not, the response is one of incredulity.

Very often they say, "Well, yes, I've thought about it and I decided against it."

"Why was that?"

"I wasn't called."

I discover that nine times out of ten, the people who feel they haven't had a call have no idea what the call is they haven't had. I have a very simple question to ask them. "If you don't know what it is, how do you know you haven't had it?" This is the mysticism with which we approach God's plan and I think that very, very often it is a mysticism that we enjoy because we love to live in the mists of it. If it becomes clear, we might have to do it.

God's will is not mystical at all; it is excruciatingly practical. This is how it works, as I understand it. Number one, God has a plan for my life. Number two, God made me. Number three, God is not stupid. Now let's go over that again, for there's some solid theology here. God has a plan for my life. God created me. God is not stupid. Therefore, God must have made me fundamentally ideal for what He wants me to do. If God has made me fundamentally ideal for what He wants me to do, perhaps the best way to find out what He wants me to do is to find out how He made me. Instead of mystically waiting for organ music, a sound like a waterfall, lights flashing in the sky, and a big bass voice intoning your name, how about getting practical?

Get a big yellow legal pad. Must be yellow; must be legal. Make a list of how God made you. Get a handle on your heritage. Get a handle on your abilities. Get a handle on your likes and on your dislikes. Get a handle on your experience. Once you've completed your list, check it out with someone who knows you well, then together look for things that need to be done, that fit the kind of person you are. Finally, have a go at it!

I can speak this with tremendous enthusiasm and conviction because in quite a similar way I discovered God's plan for me was that I should preach.

I was standing at the back of the church when a man came up to me and asked, "How old are you?"

"I'm seventeen," I answered.

"It's time you were preaching."

"I can't preach."

"Have you ever tried?"

"No."

"Well," he said, "if you've never tried, how can you possibly know you can't do it?" Then he added, "You will preach a week from Tuesday. And your subject is the church at Ephesus."

At that moment, I did not even know they had a church at Ephesus! Nevertheless, the next ten days were spent in preparation. I prepared and prepared and prepared and then I got up to speak. They gave me twenty-five minutes. I didn't dare look up until I had finished my first point. Thirty-five minutes had elapsed. I didn't know what to do. I blurted out, "I'm terribly sorry. I don't know how to stop."

Then an elderly chap in the back row gave me advice which I have consistently ignored ever since. "Well, shut up and sit down."

But the man who got me preaching came up and said, "You didn't finish, did you?"

"No," I replied.

"Finish it next Tuesday," he consoled.

Then he arranged for me to go to a little church that

didn't have a pastor. (The reason they didn't have a pastor was that they didn't have a congregation!) Then he arranged for another church and another and another. There were lots of little churches around with three or four or five people in the congregation. No preacher, nobody to go to them. So this seventeen-year-old kid started going to them, telling them about the church at Ephesus. Then when I got around the whole circuit, someone said, "Why don't you get another talk?" So I did, this time from the Old Testament. Thirty-nine years later and I haven't stopped yet.

And that's how I found God's plan for my life. Nothing very dramatic, mystical, or unusual. Actually very simple, basic, and practical. First, I learned how God had made me and what I could do. Next, I started off doing it badly. I continued doing it badly until I began to do it better. As I began to do it better, I discovered a tremendous joy in doing it. As I discovered a tremendous joy in doing it, I began to discover God's blessing resting upon it. And as time went on and God's blessing was evidently resting upon it, I began to discover the approval of God's people toward it and I knew I was in God's plan.

There's a saying abroad in the church of Jesus Christ that has probably hindered more spiritual work than any other. It goes: "If a thing's worth doing, it's worth doing well." Why does that hinder people? Because they know they can't do it well, so they don't do it at all. I have a much better approach. "If a thing's worth doing, it's worth doing badly." Anybody can do it badly. Just imagine how many people we could mobilize on that basis.

The crucial thing about my approach is allowing people to do badly only on a very limited basis at first. It's called damage control. People will start doing things badly, but it's amazing how they improve with practice; they begin to make discoveries, they begin to delight in their achievements. God is given opportunity to bless their work and the church is given opportunity to affirm it. But if they never start doing it badly, nothing, but nothing, can happen. Of course, the other possibility is that they start doing it badly and slowly get worse. What happens then? In the end, someone sitting there will say, "For goodness sake, let *me* do it." Either way, somebody discovers God's plan.

Some time ago Ray Stedman wrote a book called *Body Life*, about the church and the spiritual gifts of its people. I was talking to Ray about it and told him, "Ray, you have done a great service to the Christian church by writing *Body Life*, but many people are suffering under a misconception. They think that the Apostle Paul wrote the epistles to the Romans, the Corinthians, and the Ephesians after he read *Body Life*. They don't seem to understand that all that was there all along. The Bible has been saying all along that all believers are gifted for ministry."

Up until Ray pointed out these longstanding truths, most churches treated their ministers a little lower than the angels. They were high and elevated and remote from the people, and churches were designed for spectating. But then a change took place. People began to sense a oneness, an openness, that we're all gifted, that we could all do something. We all got excited about finding out about our gifts. Then it backfired on us. Before, when we used to ask people to do things, they'd say, "Oh, no, I couldn't." But now, since they've discovered their gifts, we ask them to do something and they respond, "That's not *my* gift." It's truly amazing how specialized people have become in the knowledge of gifts!

The Bible says that some people have the gift of faith. Does that mean that all believers don't exercise faith? No. Everybody exercises faith. It's just that some have a sharpened focus in the gift of faith. The Bible says that some people have the gift of evangelism. Does that mean only gifted evangelists evangelize? No. The Bible says all believers are witnesses. The Bible says that some people have the gift of giving. You say, "Great. I don't have that one." Well, no, the Bible doesn't say that some are gifted for giving, therefore, they are the only ones who should give.

What does it say? Everybody gives. It's just that some have a sharper focus in this area.

I confess I have never attended a seminar to discover my spiritual gift, because, frankly, I don't care what my gift is. I'm far more interested in what my ministry is. And, as far as that's concerned, I know what my ministry is. I also know that if it is my God-given ministry, then I am God-equipped to do it. Therefore, I don't need to worry about identifying my gifts or carefully examining them, and especially, I don't need to be comparing them. All I need to do is to get in there and get on with it. I can even do it badly, as long as I'm going on to discover how God made me, what He made me for, and am doing something about it.

Do you have a feel for God's plan for your life? Do you rejoice in it because you're filled with the knowledge of His will? That doesn't mean that you know everything. It doesn't mean you know the day you'll die. It doesn't mean you know the person you'll marry. It doesn't mean you'll know how many children you're going to have. It does mean that you have a real sense of God directing you in the way that you should go. Because of that servant spirit, your life is channeled, and you're serving God's purpose. I know of nothing more thrilling than to be a person serving God's purpose.

THE APPLICATION OF A SERVANT SPIRIT

Reading again in Acts 13:36, we find that "when David had served God's purpose *in his own generation,* he fell asleep" (italics added). Have you ever noticed how the older we get the more nostalgic we become? How many of you have talked about "the good old days" recently? Did you ever stop to wonder what the people in those good old days talked about? They talked about the good old days. And what about the people in the good old good old days? Eventually we end up in the Garden of Eden, and we all remember what happened there. Remember? The good old days. What was that? Getting kicked out of Eden? I submit that nostalgia trips are usually carefully induced fantasies to assist us in avoiding the present, or at least the reality of the present.

Let's take a good, long, hard look at the present. Our generation. That's a hard thing to do. I was born in 1930. I became fifty in 1980. If I continue this relentless progress, I will be seventy in the year 2000. Having thus shared my personal testimony with you, let me apply it. When I was born in 1930, there were 2 billion people on the face of the earth. Two billion in 1930. Do you know how many there were in 1980? There were 4 billion. If I live until I'm seventy, there will be 6 billion. It took from the beginning of time to 1930 to manufacture the first 2 billion. It took fifty years for the next 2 billion. It'll take twenty years for the next 2 billion, and who knows how many we'll have by the year 2025! The reason I draw these statistics to your attention is this: the church of Jesus Christ needs people with a servant spirit channeled into a sense of God's purpose relevant to our generation. If we aren't thinking in terms of the immensity of the world opportunity, and if we're not thinking in terms of the immensity of the world need, we're not thinking about serving God's purpose in our generation.

J.B. Phillips wrote a book called *Your God Is Too Small*. I suggest that many Christians today need a book called *Your Vision Is Too Small*, because it so often extends very, very little beyond the tips of our evangelical noses. If we're to serve God's purpose in our own generation, let's think in terms of the world's population. Let's think in terms of the excruciating depletion of the world's resources, particularly food and fresh water. The famine and the drought throughout the globe are obscene and unbelievably cruel. And that's our generation.

It's not all gloomy, of course. The potential for our generation is phenomenal. Recently I was in Canada to appear on the television show "One Hundred Huntley Street." It was just a simple studio, and we sat in some easy chairs and talked for twenty minutes. The interesting thing about it, however, was that the cameras were picking up that signal, beaming it off a satellite, and covering all of Canada, just like that. I was sitting in a chair, covering Canada. And to cover Canada means going from the Maritime Provinces across Quebec and Ontario, through the great prairie states, and finally British Columbia, right out to the Island of Victoria. It goes from Atlantic to Pacific, from sea to shining sea, but almost twice as far across as the United States. And that's our generation.

So, in other words, if we're going to be realistic about engendering a spiritual attitude, a Christian attitude, we need to begin to discover what it means to serve, what it means to serve God's purpose, and to put it into the whole context of the unique opportunities, privileges, and responsibilities of being part of this generation. Do you know why? Because future generations can't serve this one—only we can.

Ask yourself these questions: Do I see a servant spirit developing within me? Do I see it sharply focused in terms of God's purpose? Is it relevant to the contemporary scene of which I'm a part? This is what I mean by the servant spirit. This is what I mean by Christian motivation. It is so different from everything we see around us.

THE RESULTS OF A SERVANT SPIRIT

Our text says, "When David had served God's purpose in his own generation, *he fell asleep*" (italics added). Theologians tell us that the expression *he fell asleep* is a Hebraic euphemism. In layman's language, a euphemism is a figure of speech that substitutes an inoffensive expression for one that is offensive. We take an unpleasant situation and dress it up a bit.

I was brought up in a small church where a fellow named Willie Peel used to give the announcements. His trousers were always short and he always walked with his feet at 2 and 10 o'clock. It was very intriguing for a young boy to sit and watch this man, Willie Peel. Willie never got his "h's" in the right place. For instance, he'd always give the "hannouncements." He also used euphemisms all the time. Wilie wouldn't recognize a euphemism if he bumped into it, but that was what he did. Nobody ever was taken ill in our church. They were "laid on one side in a bed of sickness." That used to conjure up the most gruesome pictures in my mind. For the rest of the service I would wonder why someone didn't reach out and turn the old lady over. That's a euphemism. Nobody ever died—they were always "called home," "went to their reward," or "departed this life."

Back to David. When David had served God's purpose in his own generation, he dropped dead. That's what it literally means. But it sounds much nicer to say falling asleep, doesn't it? There's more to it than that, however.

The idea of falling asleep implies waking up. After all of us have lived and fallen asleep, we will wake up and see the Lord. And He will say, "While I was on earth I didn't come to be served, but to serve. Tell Me, what was your approach?"

There are, of course, two answers to that question. One is, "I guess I didn't come to serve, but to be served." The other is, "Well, Lord, when I discovered who You are and what You'd done, I was so grateful that I committed my life to serving You. Whatever I did, I tried to do it heartily and as to the Lord. Because I knew I served You, Lord Christ, I had a tremendous desire to discover and do Your will. I failed so often, and I'm mortified by the way that I've failed. But You know my heart, Lord. My overriding desire was to develop that servant spirit to serve You."

To such a profession, Jesus will say, "Well done. Well done, good and faithful servant." That is the highest accolade we can aim for. There's nothing nobler. What a lovely thing it would be if from now until the day we fall asleep, we could say out of sheer gratitude, "Lord Jesus, teach me the servant spirit."

"When David had served God's purpose in his own generation, he fell asleep," was Paul's approving summary of the great king's career. And certainly the great apostle was made of the same stuff because he did not hesitate to say of himself, "Though I am free and belong to no man, I make myself a slave [a servant] to everyone, to win as many as possible" (1 Corinthians 9:19).

PERSONAL REFLECTION

Gracious Father, what a privilege it is to know You, what a thrill it is to be confronted with Your awesome holiness, Your majesty, Your glory. What a joy it is to be confronted with Your righteousness, Your purity, and then to know that You're knowable through Your Son, our Lord Jesus. I recognize that You're only knowable through His sacrifice; You're only knowable because He did not think that trappings of majesty should be held onto, but He humbled Himself and accepted the servant's role. It is only because of His servanthood that I know You.

Blessed Lord Jesus, thank You so much for showing me Your servanthood, for You served both the Father and a needy race. Thank You for reminding me that those who would follow You should emulate Your example and generate Your attitude.

Gracious Father, point out within my heart my selfishness, my arrogance, my apathy. Reveal within my soul my unwholesome ambition. Show me my weaknesses and how they can be rectified. Give me that overriding desire, whatever I do, to be a servant of the living God. Help me to work toward that day when, falling asleep, I will stand before You and hear from Your lips that which will set me right for eternity: "Well done, good and faithful servant."

"If others have this right of support from you, shouldn't we have it all the more?

"But we did not use this right. On the contrary, we put up with anything rather than hinder the Gospel of Christ. Don't you know that those who work in the temple get their food from the temple, and those who serve at the altar share in what is offered on the altar? In the same way, the Lord has commanded that those who preach the Gospel should receive their living from the Gospel.

"But I have not used any of these rights. And I am writing this in the hope that you will do such things for me. I would rather die than have anyone deprive me of this boast. Yet when I preach the Gospel, I cannot boast, for I am compelled to preach. Woe to me if I do not preach the Gospel! If I preach voluntarily, I have a reward; if not voluntarily, I am simply discharging the trust committed to me. What then is my reward? Just this: that in preaching the Gospel I may offer it free of charge, and so not make use of my rights in preaching it."

1 CORINTHIANS 9:12-18

three
WHEN DUTY CALLS

It would be absolutely marvelous if every morning we got up motivated by the gratitude attitude to such an extent that we began to demonstrate the servant spirit. But probably, if we're honest with ourselves, we have to admit that it doesn't always work out that way. I wonder why?

Some of us men wake up in the morning, look at our wives sleeping peacefully beside us, and say to ourselves, "There she lies. She had all the world to choose from and she chose me. I am so thankful. For twenty years she has unselfishly given of herself to me. She has cared for me. She has borne my children. She has borne my problems. She has dealt with my finances. She has looked after the household. She is an absolute wonder. I am so grateful that I will leap out of bed and make breakfast for her." Right? Why are we laughing? Because it doesn't work out that way, and we don't expect it to. Why not? Basically, because we're selfish. And that's why it is necessary for God to build other motivational factors into our lives.

Scripture clearly indicates that we Christians are *sometimes* motivated by the gratitude attitude and *sometimes* motivated by the servant spirit, but not *always*. That does not mean, however, that we are free to be unmotivated. It's quite possible that some of you read chapters 1 and 2 and said to yourselves, "Well, I just don't have this gratitude attitude. I'm just naturally a bit of a grouch. And I don't buy this servant spirit stuff. So I guess I don't need to worry about it." Don't let yourself off the hook so quickly.

Even when these two motivational factors are not at work, a sense of duty should be. Every mature person recognizes that in this life certain duties are required of him. And the Christian in particular should have a keen sense of *Christian duty.*

THE QUESTION OF RIGHTS

The Apostle Paul is a man most parents, sales people, teachers, and preachers can identify with because he advocates a very sound learning principle: *if you want to make a point, repeat it until it sinks in.* In 1 Corinthians 9:20-22, Paul makes his point, then starts multiplying illustrations of it until he picks up a rhythm: "To the Jews I became like a Jew, to win the Jews. To those under the Law I became like one under the Law . . . so as to win those under the Law. To those not having the Law I became like one not having the Law . . . so as to win those not having the Law. To the weak I became weak, to win the weak."

Reading the text fully, we notice Paul twice inserts parenthetical phrases to qualify what he has just said. It's the second parenthetical phrase, found in verse 21, that I want to focus on here. Paul says, "I became like one not having the Law (though I am not free from God's law but am under Christ's law)." In other words, he, as a believer in the Gospel, recognizes that Christians come under the law of Christ.

When we come under the law of Christ, we begin to recognize that we live in a relationship with Him, and part of that relationship is a recognition of our responsibility to Christ and our ultimate accountability to Him. We have a sense of duty to the Lord Jesus, and that becomes a prime motivating factor. In our society, however, there isn't much emphasis on duty. There isn't much emphasis on responsibility and accountability.

In 1805 Admiral Lord Nelson sailed his intrepid British fleet to engage the French and Spaniards at the Battle of Trafalgar. At the start of the fight, he ran up a signal on his flagship, *Victory*, which said, "England expects every man to do his duty." And as he later that same day lay dying on the deck of *Victory*, wounded by a sharpshooter from an enemy ship, he said, "Thank God, I have done my duty." Here was a man with a tremendous sense of responsibility and accountability to his nation. He expected all the men of his fleet to have that same feeling, and when he died, he wasn't bemoaning his death; he was glad that he had done his duty. People once had a tremendous sense of duty to the state, to the authorities over them. To a large extent, that is not true today.

An even more encompassing call to duty is found in Solomon's words recorded in Ecclesiastes 12:13: "Fear God and keep His commandments, for this is the whole duty of man." This defines a sense of responsibility even beyond that to king and country. It declares an allegiance or moral obligation to God Himself. But here again, this type of devotion is sadly lacking today.

In fact, if people do have a sense of duty in our society, it is likely to be a sense of duty to themselves alone. Their driving concern is their own well-being, their own happiness, their own comfort, their own pleasure. Of course, if we have a society of people primarily interested in their own pleasure, and if the only duty they see is to themselves—not to king and country, not to God, not to neighbor, but exclusively to themselves—it's rather obvious that we have some major problems. The tragedy of the whole thing, as far as believers are concerned, is that this attitude has infiltrated the Christian community as well. If we're more concerned about individual rights and individual freedoms than corporate duty, then we will have difficulty within the body of Christ.

Be that as it may, Paul doesn't suggest for a moment that rights are unimportant. On the contrary, he says that rights must be recognized, and from the very beginning of 1 Corinthians 9, he points out that, because he is an apostle, he has certain rights. One of the rights he mentions is the right to be recognized by these infant churches as an apostle in whom very specific authority resides and upon whom certain responsibilities rest (verses 1-2). In verses 3-6, he points out his right to be respected as a human being: "Don't we have the right to food and drink? Don't we have the right to take a believing wife along with us, as do the other apostles and the Lord's brothers and Cephas? Or is it only I and Barnabas who must work for a living?" In verses 7-12, he uses many arguments to show that he has every right to be remunerated for his work as a minister. So when the Apostle Paul talks about duty to the Lord Jesus, he is not suggesting for a moment that there are no such things as individual rights.

THE QUESTION OF RESPONSIBILITY

What then is Paul saying? Simply this: that although individual rights must be recognized, they must also be carefully regulated.

I believe the Scripture teaches that rights are secondary to responsibilities. To see what I mean, carefully examine the Ten Commandments sometime and you'll discover very little about human rights and very much about human responsibilities. Yet inherent in these great statements of human responsibility is a clear connection to human rights. For instance, the human responsibility is, "Thou shalt not kill." God could have said, "You have the inalienable right to life." But He didn't focus on the right. He focused instead on the responsibility. But interestingly enough, if people fulfill the responsibility, guess what happens? Another person's rights are met. The only way that my right to life can be preserved and protected is by other people respecting me and accepting the responsibility not to kill me. Another example: the human responsibility is, "Thou shalt not steal." Now, of course, God could have said, "You have the inalienable right to property." He didn't, but He's saying the same thing. I only have the right to amass property when other people recognize their responsibility not to steal from me.

Not only are rights linked to responsibility but the Apostle Paul tells us here in 1 Corinthians 9 that rights are *always* subject to restraint. Three times he speaks from his own experience: "We did not use this right" (verse 12). "I have not used any of these rights" (verse 15). "So [I do] not make use of my rights in preaching it [the Gospel]" (verse 18). "Yes, I've got my rights," he insists, "but all my rights are regulated by a prior commitment to my responsibilities."

It's very important that we get this concept in a biblical balance because I feel there is an imbalance in our society. People have a strong commitment to their individual rights without recognizing that these rights can only become true and real with a commitment to responsibility. The mature Christian accepts responsibility as primary and rights as secondary. And he also recognizes that his primary responsibility is to live under the law of Christ. That means living by Christ's dictates, under His control. We must have a sense of duty toward Him.

When we talk in terms of living under the law of Christ, we must recognize that Paul speaks of the law in a number of different ways. For instance, in Romans 8:2 he says, "The law of the Spirit of life [in Christ Jesus has] set me free from the law of sin and death." We are all born with a downward gravitational pull that biases us toward selfishness and sinfulness. The problem is that sin leads to death—spiritual death, physical death, eternal death.

The essence of the Christian Gospel, however, is this: the law of the Spirit of life in Christ Jesus has set us free from the law of sin and death. God has introduced into our lives in Christ a new law, a new principle—called the law of the Spirit of life—which counteracts the old one and sets us free.

Now, if that sounds complicated, just think of a very simple illustration. Let's say you want to travel to New York. You go to the airport, sit in the plane, fasten your seat belt, and earnestly try to defy gravity. You can't do it. Gravity is too strong for you. It will hold you down and keep you from getting to New York. If, however, the pilot switches on the engines and there's enough fuel in the tanks, the law of aerodynamics will suddenly begin to take over and surge through the airplane. Soon, you will be set free from the law of gravity. You will take off and land in the Big Apple.

Now, then, in exactly the same way, when you find yourself in Christ, the Spirit of the living God moves into your life. And when He does, He counteracts the downward gravitational pull of sin and death. The Spirit sets you free.

What does He set you free for? To please yourself? To do as you wish? No. For Paul, in Romans 8, tells us: "The law of the Spirit of life [in Christ Jesus] set me free from the law of sin and death . . . in order that the righteous requirements of the law might be fully met in us, who do not live according to the sinful nature but according to the Spirit" (verses 2, 4). You are not set free to please yourself but to fulfill the righteousness of the law. In other words, you are set free to live under the power of the Spirit, fulfilling a sense of duty, of responsibility, of accountability to the Lord Jesus whose you are and whom you serve. That's why the Apostle Paul says, "I've got lots of rights, folks, but far more important than my rights is my responsibility. And my responsibility is clear-cut: having been set free by the Spirit of life, I am now able to serve the Lord Jesus Christ. I am His and His alone." Now we begin to discover the source of his sense of duty.

Do you find yourself breathing the atmosphere of our secular world? Do you find yourself more concerned about preserving and protecting your rights than about fulfilling your responsibilities? Do you find yourself motivated by a tremendous desire to honor the Lord Jesus Christ under whose law you operate? Or do you find yourself constantly being pulled back into doing your own thing, pleasing yourself, going as you wish through life? I encourage you to realize that the Spirit of the living God has set you free from the old life in order that you might come under the law of Christ and sense your duty toward Him. But how does this work out?

First of all, the Apostle Paul tells us that coming under the law of Christ triggers a sense of compulsion. "When I preach the Gospel, I cannot boast, for I am compelled to preach" (1 Corinthians 9:16).

The Greek word Paul uses here is the same found in Matthew 14:22, where the Lord Jesus tells the disciples to get into the boat and go on ahead of Him to the other side of the lake. Let me re-create the scene:

Peter protests Christ's command to sail: "Master, there's a storm coming!"

And Jesus says, "So?"

"So it is very dangerous to be out in the middle of the lake in this little boat. If You were a fisherman, You'd understand that, Master, but You're a carpenter turned preacher. So why don't You stick to carpentry and preaching, and let me handle the boats and the storms and the fish. We're not going."

And the Lord Jesus said, "Get in the boat."

Peter held his ground. "We don't want to get in the boat."

"I don't remember asking you if you wanted to get in the boat."

"It would not be advisable."

"I'm not discussing the advisability either."

"Let's take a vote," Peter suggested, frantically hoping to get the support of the rest of the disciples.

At that point Jesus puts His foot in His voice and booms, "GET IN THE BOAT!" And there's something about what He said and the way He said it that made all these fellows, against their better judgment, jump in the boat and row straight out into the storm. That's motivation!

It's a sense of motivation, however, that is singularly lacking among many believers today. The Lord Jesus compelled the Apostle Paul to preach. He compelled Peter and the other disciples to get in the boat. I wonder what the Lord Jesus does in terms of compelling His people today? And are we so convinced of His lordship, so committed to operating under His law, that we recognize He doesn't discuss or debate or take a vote; He simply tells us what to do and we jump to it and do it?

Paul goes on to say this: "Woe to me if I do not preach the Gospel!" Now most of us assume that the Apostle Paul just loved to preach. We figure he couldn't wait to find a crowd of people. His eyes would begin to glisten and we can imagine him licking his lips, limbering his preaching finger, getting three points in mind, and saying, "Oh, boy, here we go. Let's get to it!" But it just isn't necessarily so.

When you go to work and are faced with a desk-load of mail, don't you ever pick it up and say, "If I see another pile of mail like this, I'm going to scream"? Do you young moms ever look at that growing pile of diapers and say, "If I see another diaper, I'm going to scream"? And what about preachers? They say to themselves sometimes, "If I see another congregation, just one more congregation, and I have to think in terms of one more sermon and three more points, I'm going to scream!" Apostles, business people, moms, and preachers—we're all alike.

This is where another factor comes into the picture. The Lord Jesus says, in essence, "I didn't ask you if you felt like it. I didn't ask you if you're excited about it, and I didn't ask you if you felt receptive. Actually, I didn't ask you anything. I simply told you to get on with it. And, by the way, if you don't, you're in trouble. Woe be to you." There's a keen sense of accountability in the person who ministers in the name of Christ. In many instances, however, this keen sense of accountability is just not there.

Several ushers at our church confided to me that some men say they will "ush" (or whatever it is that ushers do) and when the time comes for them to "ush," they don't show. One of the nursery supervisors recently told me, "We had a lot of people committed to working in the nursery this week, but they just didn't show." It seems to me perfectly reasonable to expect that when people come into a church to worship, there will be somebody to greet them, somebody to help them find a seat, somebody to care for their small children. But how on earth is that going to be done if someone won't accept the responsibilities for those activities, if someone only does his job when he feels like it?

Jesus deals with *all* His disciples the same in this regard—be they 1st-century or 20th-century. When once in a while we don't feel like doing what we're supposed to do, He compels us to do it anyway. Furthermore, when we still don't want to do it, He says, "I'll hold you accountable if you don't." And that's motivation.

A psychologist once told me that sometimes we have to work out our fantasies, so I have decided to tell you mine. You may not be particularly interested, but bear with me. Here's my fantasy: I think it's going to snow before long. And it's going to snow on a Saturday night. Sunday morning the alarm is going to go off, and I'm going to go to the window, look outside, and see the beautiful white snow that the loving Lord has sent. And I'm going to say, "Amen, hallelujah, praise God," and jump straight back in the sack. Now this is only the beginning of the fantasy.

Twenty-five minutes after eight, the phone will ring. "Hello, Stuart Briscoe here."

"Stuart, where are you?"

"I'm talking to you."

"Well, what do you mean, you're talking to me?"

"You just dialed my number, didn't you?"

"Yes. Do you know what day it is?"

"Sunday. I even know what time it is—8:25."

"Do you know what that means?"

"Yes, the first service will start in five minutes, and I'm in bed."

"Well, what are you going to do?"

"Well, we're going to have to trust in the Lord." (That's a spiritual answer to a practical problem.)

"I'm serious!"

"Well, we've got twelve pastors; call one of them. I didn't feel led to come this morning."

"That's what we did: we called them, and you won't believe what happened! They don't feel led either."

Now, what I don't divulge, you see, is that we pastors decided on this plan the previous Monday. We decided that we don't want to feel distant from the congregation. We want the congregation to feel that we're part of them. As long as we all feel the same, we're all of the same motivation, and we just won't go to church when it snows.

I don't worry too much about my fantasy happening, because I know we're not going to do it. And I'll tell you why we're not going to do it. The Lord Jesus, who told His disciples to get in the boat, says to me and each of our pastors on Sunday mornings, "Get out of that bed." He also says that to a lot of other disciples who won't listen. And therein lies their lack of motivation, their lack of old-time, old-fashioned, delightful sense of duty and commitment to our Lord Jesus.

You can always tell people who put responsibilities ahead of rights and who put the responsibility of serving the Lord Christ ahead of other responsibilities. You can identify them because they do what they've committed themselves to do as unto the Lord. That's Christian motivation. That's what sets Christians apart, and if that motivation is absent, then, quite frankly, we believers will be totally indistinguishable from secular society. The salt will have lost its saltiness. The light will be hidden under a bucket.

But not only that, the Apostle Paul adds that those who come under the Lord Christ also have a sense of reward: "If I preach voluntarily, I have a reward; if not voluntarily, I am simply discharging the trust committed to me" (1 Corinthians 9:17). There are two ways I can do it. I can preach and fulfill my ministry voluntarily, or I can do it involuntarily. If I do it voluntarily, I have a reward.

There is a real sense of reward involving Christian motivation. Now some people say, "Oh, that's all wrong." Wait just a minute. There's a great thrill in knowing that we're going to be rewarded by the Lord Jesus for the simple reason that it brings Him such delight. There's nothing that will thrill the Lord Jesus more than to tell one of His loyal children, "Well done, good and faithful servant." Imagine the pleasure in the Lord's voice as He says it. Imagine His excitement as He takes a crown and places it on the faithful servant's head. Let's not be too picky about this reward business; we never are in any other area—why should we be in this? Particularly if we recognize that it is something that comes from the heart of the Lord. Besides, the Bible teaches us that we're not going to keep our heavenly crowns on our heads very long, because we're going to be throwing them at His feet.

I remember talking to a young girl one day who said, "I've just been thinking about going to heaven. I don't know what the glassy sea is that the Book of Revelation talks about and I don't know who will be in that big crowd with all those folks sitting around, but I do know I'm going to get a crown. And I know I'm going to take off my crown and send it skimming across that glassy sea, then do cartwheels to the glory of God."

I don't know what your vision of heaven is, but I rather liked hers. If heaven is nothing more than playing harps, I'm not too enthusiastic about it. I like the idea of skimming crowns across the glassy sea and doing cartwheels and feeling exhilaration and excitement. But I'm sure there will be some people in heaven with no cartwheels, no crown, nothing to throw, no excitement at all. They will have been saved by the skin of their teeth. They never experienced the earthly joy of coming under the law of Christ and honoring

Him. What a tragedy! What a shame!

The Scriptures talk about a sense of compulsion, a sense of accountability, and yes, a sense of reward. But the Scriptures also talk about a sense of trust. Paul says in effect, "Sometimes I'll do the ministry involuntarily. I'll do it when I don't feel like it, and I'll do it when I don't want to. The lovely thing about it is that I'll do it because I'll be trusted to do it." Very often we trust people who in turn let us down, but these verses speak of trust in a nobler sense—that of the Lord Jesus trusting *us* to serve *Him.* While it's bad when we let each other down, the real tragedy is when we let Him down. And that is another factor that motivates us as we come under the law of Christ.

Let's review for a moment. We understand about our rights. We hear about them all the time. They're even implied in Scripture. We have our rights because we're people of dignity created in the image of God. God wants us to have our rights fully met, but He wants us to recognize, first and foremost, the correct emphasis is on responsibility and a sense of duty to Him. The question I want us to ask ourselves right now is this: is that what we're doing? Is that how we're operating? Is that what is really happening in our lives?

THE QUESTION OF RESULTS

What are the results of living under the law of Christ? First of all is a sense of *durability.* In 1 Corinthians 9:12 Paul says, "If others have this right of support from you, shouldn't we have it all the more? But we did not use this right. [Now listen to this marvelous sentence.] On the contrary, we put up with anything rather than hinder the Gospel of Christ." Now the Apostle Paul could have said, "I've had it with these Corinthians. They're the most thankless lot I've ever met. I've poured myself into them and all I've gotten in return is a lot of heat. They won't even recognize my apostleship, and if it weren't for me exercising my apostleship, they wouldn't even be believers. Forget it. There are plenty of other places to go." But Paul realizes such an attitude would not be right. "I have a sense of duty to the Lord for those people, and I'm going to stick with it. And I'm going to maintain my ministry among them. I'll put up with anything for the sake of the Gospel of Christ."

What would you put up with for the sake of your Christian service? Are you, like Paul, prepared to suffer when you don't have to? Are you, like Paul, willing to serve where you don't want to? Don't run away with the idea that there's such a glorious motivation on the part of some people that they never struggle and it's never a battle and there are never choices to be made. Recognize instead that all of those under the law of Christ will battle against selfishness. All of us will battle against a variety of competing demands and motivational factors. Yet a sense of duty to Christ must exist if we're to be durable, tough, and able to follow through.

Second, if we truly live under the law of Christ, we will have a sense of *expendability*. "What then is my reward?" asks Paul. "Just this: that in preaching the Gospel I may offer it free of charge, and so not make use of my rights in preaching it" (1 Corinthians 9:18). In other words, he's saying, "Listen, folks, I have my rights, but I'm not going to insist on them. In fact, I would rather just forget about these rights than detract from what I'm trying to do."

In our own areas of ministry, how many times do other considerations push in? How often do personal concerns become more important than the Lord and the people we serve? And how often do we get sidetracked? Expendable people will say no when selfishness rears its head. Expendable people will say yes to servanthood. And then they'll stick with it when they feel there's absolutely no encouragement or reward. How can they do it? Because they've come under the law of Christ.

Third, when we submit to the law of Christ, we experience a sense of *flexibility*. When people become inflexible, very often it's because they've lost sight of the long-range goal. They become locked into doing things a certain way, thus limiting themselves, and lose the vision of what *Christ* is doing and what He wants them to do. The Apostle Paul puts it beautifully: "I have become all things to all men so that by all possible means I might save some" (1 Corinthians 9:22). It's sad that this verse is often used by politicians as a slur. When they said it of Jimmy Carter they meant that he was spineless and flip-flopping all over the place. That's a gross misquotation of Scripture, for what the Apostle Paul is saying is this: "When I come under the law of Christ, serving Him, fulfilling what He wants me to do, then His cause becomes so important that it eliminates all my rigidity. It erases all my narrowness and extinguishes all my bigotry. I become a flexible person in His hands, because the important thing is doing my duty to Him, serving the Lord."

What a joy it is to see someone with a flexible attitude. Paul says he's prepared to work with *all* men. Isn't that delightful? I've noticed in Christian service we have a tendency to become more and more specialized. Some folks say, "Well, I only want to work with women." Or, "I only want to work with young women who live in the suburbs." Or, "Sharp, young men, that's who I want to work with." Or, "I want to work with kids."

"All right. What kind of kids? Kids in the ghetto?"

"Oh, no, I don't have a feel for that kind of kids."

The Apostle Paul didn't operate like this at all. He said, "I am a debtor both to Greeks and to barbarians, both to wise and to unwise" (Romans 1:14, NKJV). *Wise* and *unwise* are two interesting words in this passage. *Wise* is the Greek *sophos* and *unwise* is *moron.* You don't need to know much Greek to know what he's getting at. The Apostle Paul says, "I don't care if they're Jews or Greeks." That's a Jew talking! He says, "I don't care if they're sophisticated or blockheads." So let's be done with this inflexibility. Let's be done with the specialized way we're doing things. Instead, let's get excited about our duty to the Lord Jesus and serving Him any way, anywhere, anytime.

Admiral Lord Nelson met his own challenge at Trafalgar and could die saying, "Thank God, I've done my duty." The Lord Jesus has likewise raised a flag on the masthead of His church, exhorting every believer to do his duty. And what more exciting thing than to reach life's end, look in His wonderful face, and say, "Thank God, I did my duty." The gratitude attitude? Yes. The servant spirit? Yes. But never forget the powerful motivating factor of duty's call.

PERSONAL REFLECTION

Father, You know our hearts; You know our desires. Each of us is different. Some of us have hearts which are not particularly warm to You, which are hard to Your call. Some of us are very sensitive to You, responsive to Your call. Please take Your Word, by Your Spirit, and write it deeply on our consciences and minds. Lead us to understand what You would have us be and do.

"So then, men ought to regard us as servants of Christ and as those entrusted with the secret things of God. Now it is required that those who have been given a trust must prove faithful. I care very little if I am judged by you or by any human court; indeed, I do not even judge myself. My conscience is clear, but that does not make me innocent. It is the Lord who judges me. Therefore judge nothing before the appointed time; wait till the Lord comes. He will bring to light what is hidden in darkness and will expose the motives of men's hearts. At that time each will receive his praise from God."

1 CORINTHIANS 4:1-5

four
A SENSE OF PRIVILEGE

When I was eighteen, there was a war on in Korea. About that time I got a very nice letter from the British government saying that they would like me to try to fit that war into my agenda and suggesting I show up at a certain place to have a medical examination. Being a law-abiding citizen, I showed up for my medical examination. After breathing on a mirror to prove I was alive, I was pronounced to be in first-class physical condition and asked which armed service I wanted to join. I said I didn't particularly want to join anything—it was their idea, not mine. However, a man standing nearby in a magnificent uniform caught my eye, and so I asked, "What's he?"

"He's a Royal Marine."

"OK, I'll join them."

And though it may be difficult to believe, that was my motivation for joining the Marines. I just liked the uniform.

It's amazing what uniforms do for people. You can take a man and dress him in a sweatshirt and jeans and he's just a man in a sweatshirt and jeans. Put him in a uniform, though, and he suddenly becomes a different person, one with a high sense of identification and privilege. He really feels that he belongs. And consequently, he begins to move in a different manner.

I was with Cliff Barrows one day as he busily attended to the many preparatory details for a series of evangelistic meetings. Soon a little lady came up to him, wanting to reminisce about the times they had sung together. It was obvious that Cliff hadn't the remotest idea who the woman was, so I maneuvered her gently to one side and chatted while he got on with what he was trying to do. What I discovered was that her idea of singing with Cliff Barrows was that she had been a member of his 10,000-voice choir in a football stadium and once had actually been within 125 feet of him! But for her, the big thing was that she had identified with his group. She felt privileged to be part of it, and had never forgotten it. It had been the greatest time of her life.

I don't wish to underestimate the sense of privilege that people can have by identifying with certain causes or individuals. So often it will make them behave in a way they've never behaved before or perform in a manner far greater, far richer, than they were ever able to before. And this is certainly true of Christians as well, who are privileged to be identified with the greatest cause in the world.

The Apostle Paul, as 1 Corinthians 4 makes quite obvious, is having a hard time with the believers of Corinth. Many of them aren't particularly impressed with him. Some don't like the way he preaches. Others don't like the things that he preaches. Some don't like his appearance. A few question whether he is an apostle at all. One group wants him to come back. Others don't ever want to see him again. Yet Paul is trying to mold this Corinthian church into a cohesive group, attempting to get them all to agree on something. And it's rather interesting to notice that the common thread he uses here is privilege: "Can't we agree about our privileged position? Can't we let that get a grip on us and motivate us so we can all begin to move in the same direction?"

THE MATTER OF POSITION

First of all, Paul says, "Let's regard ourselves as servants of Christ," then, secondly, "as those entrusted with the secret things of God" (1 Corinthians 4:1). In other words, he says all Christians should recognize they possess positions of privilege.

The Greek word translated *servant* in this passage was used to describe a person who simply existed to fulfill the wishes of his principal. For example, when John Mark traveled with Paul and Barnabas on their first missionary journey, it says in the *King James Version* that he went as their minister. That doesn't mean to say that he held Sunday morning worship services for them, only that he handled all the necessary paperwork. He went to the embassies to get their visas. He made sure their passport photographs were right. He checked on their airline tickets. He handled all their hotel reservations. John Mark's sole responsibility was to ensure that the desires and wishes of Paul and Barnabas were met. That is the idea behind *huperetes*.

Another interesting usage of the word is found in the Gospels when the Lord Jesus on one occasion said, "If someone takes you to court, agree before you get there. Settle out of court." (Good advice, incidentally, but that's not our subject.) In modern vernacular, He said, "If you don't, they'll probably take you to the cleaners. If you do go to court," Christ continued, "there's a high probability that the judge will find against you and commit you to the *huperetes.*" But here it's translated *jailer.* Now the jailer doesn't decide what's going to happen to people; the judge does that. The jailer simply exists in order that the wishes of his principal, the judge, might come to reality. Now, says the Apostle Paul, we are like the jailer to the judge. We are like John Mark to Paul. In our relationship to Jesus Christ, we have a privileged position. We have been identified with the Lord Jesus in order that we might be the practical means of His wishes coming to fruition.

The usage of *huperetes* in secular Greek also provides

insight. In ancient days the boats plying up and down the Mediterranean were propelled by men pulling on the oars. These rowers were on the lower deck and on the upper deck was the captain. The captain was the one who decided where the boat was going, when, and how fast. And the men down below just pulled on the oars. Now the captain could decide where they were going until he was blue in the face, but with nobody pulling on the oars, he didn't get there. By the same token, the men pulling on the oars could make all kinds of absolutely irrelevant decisions without effect, because it was the one on the upper deck who decided where they were going. A relationship existed, a relationship of the captain and the under-rower. In fact, the word *huperetes* is translated in secular Greek as *under-rower.*

If you want a graphic image of your relationship to Christ, it is this. You have been called by the Lord Jesus Christ to pull on the oars so that His ship of state can sail into the place of His choosing, so that He, the Captain, might accomplish what He desires.

I love that picture. I've been given my oar and you've been given your oar and we're all in the same ship, every single one of us a servant of Christ, pulling together. Let's get rid of the type of thinking that says: "I'm tired of pulling on my oar," or "Why can't I have her oar?" or "Why does she get to sit over there when I have to sit back here?" Each of us must do our job with our eyes and mind always fixed on the Man on the upper deck who is deciding where we are going. We are simply the means of facilitating His desires.

Next in 1 Corinthians 4:1 comes the privilege of knowing that we are "entrusted with the secret things of God." The *King James Version* uses a rather interesting and poetic expression: it says that we are "stewards of the mysteries."

This idea of mysteries is a little confusing in the New Testament, and I want to take just a minute to simplify it. When we think of a mystery, if we think about a mystery at all, we may think of something written by Agatha Christie, that marvelous lady who used to dream up all kinds of situations where the most unlikely people would be stuck in the most unlikely situations—with no way out.

In chapter 1, Christie would introduce her cast of characters, but by the chapter's conclusion, there would be a terrible scream and one of the lot would be found very dead. Immediately you surmise "whodunit," because of all the people you met in the first chapter, there's one obvious rogue. The problem is that by the end of the second chapter you're not sure, especially when the rogue himself is murdered. Chapter by chapter, a character is bumped off until at last you're totally confused. You have no idea who the culprit is. That's a mystery.

Unfortunately, when some people read about the mysteries in the New Testament, they think that God is like a celestial Agatha Christie, sitting up in heaven just complicating things and messing up the works. Just when they think they have one piece unraveled, they find another knot in the situation.

We need to remember that when we read the word *mystery* in the New Testament, it is a very slack, lazy piece of translation, because the Greek word *mysterion* has nothing to do with our modern concept. To us a mystery is something that is utterly confusing, beyond figuring out. The Greeks thought differently. They had mystery religions or secret societies. If you weren't a member, you had no idea what was going on. But if you were initiated into membership, everything was revealed to you. It became obvious. When the New Testament uses the word *mysterion*, it isn't talking about things you don't know; it is talking about things now revealed to you that you *previously* didn't know and that are still secret to many other people. The mysteries of God have been revealed to the initiated, says the Apostle Paul. But he then adds an admonition: those of us who have received the mysteries, who have had our eyes opened, must understand that we have received this information, this insight, as a sacred trust. We are trustees of it.

When you take your money or check into the bank, you give it to a teller. You have no idea who he or she is, but you never think for a minute that the teller will pocket the money, then go out and spend it. You know that you are entrusting it to the bank. It's your money, but they're going to accept full responsibility for administering it as you wish until you want it back again. In the same way, if the Lord Jesus has opened your eyes to truth, if you have become initiated into the mysteries of God, if God has shown Himself to you through Jesus Christ, if you've begun to grasp redemption, if you've begun to have your mind set ablaze by the Holy Spirit, it wasn't in order that you might just sit back and enjoy it. It was in order that you might be like a banker handling someone else's money, holding it in trust for him.

So that's what Paul means when he says, "We are privileged people." It is because we're part of Jesus' ship of state, pulling on our own little oars, contributing to getting Him to where He wants to be. We are privileged people because He has opened our eyes to things other people don't understand and has entrusted this information to us in order that we might do with it what *He* wishes, and ultimately, that we might disseminate it to others who don't know.

I must admit quite frankly that when I seek encouragement from the Scriptures for my own ministry I turn to this passage more than any other, because I find that the thing that gets me excited all over again, whatever else is happening, is this deep sense of privilege. I find it tremendously exhilarating to realize that God, for reasons known only to Himself, has called me and you and all of His people to be stewards of the mysteries and under-rowers of Jesus Christ.

As we look around the world today, we find many different lifestyles. And looking behind the lifestyles, we find philosophies of life. In simple terms, the way people behave is a clue to what they believe. Or to put it another way, philosophy of life is the root from which lifestyle grows.

Let's examine two fundamentally different philosophies of life and see how they fit into Paul's message to the Corinthians.

First are the people who ask philosophical questions. They usually do this during the college years, because afterward they're too busy paying the mortgage. While at State U. they ponder magnificent questions like, "Who am I? What am I? Why am I? Where did I come from? Where am I going?" And they sit up all night drinking gallons of coffee, speculating on the answers. Of course, they do go to an occasional class and there they listen to the professor speaking with tremendous authority about *his* speculations. These men and women graduate from college with all kinds of speculative answers to all kinds of immense philosophical questions. They put it all together, and it becomes their philosophy of life, from which they begin to build their lifestyle.

The problem with a speculative philosophy is that everyone is free to speculate on it—it is always "open season." So what happens? People have to go back to the drawing board and get a whole new system and work out a whole new lifestyle. That's the state of modern society; that's why there's so much change, so much uncertainty, so much insecurity.

Fortunately, there's another approach to life. It doesn't start down here on earth, but up in heaven; not with man, but with God. God leans forward on His throne and says, "Excuse Me." Now, very often, He has a hard time getting people's attention and that's why all kinds of things happen in their lives. After gentle whispers and suggestions, God is at last forced to pick up His two-by-four and say, "Excuse Me. *Now* do I have your attention?"

Once He has your attention, He says, "Now, I would like to tell you who you are, where you came from, and where you're going. And do you know how I am going to do it? I'm going to tell you who *I* am. Are you listening?"

And you say, "Yes, yes," because you see Him fingering

His two-by-four. "I've got the message. What You're doing is revealing truth to me."

Do you see the difference in life philosophies? One approach is *man* speculating about the questions of existence and coming up with his best guesses. And our society is full of the products of man's best guesses. The other approach is *God* taking the initiative and telling us the answers. The former is called speculative philosophy; the latter is called revealed theology. You can build your lifestyle on one or the other. The confusion rampant in our world today is directly attributable to speculative philosophies. The confusion rampant in many Christian lives today is that they profess to build their lives on revealed theology, but in actuality they are simply succumbing to speculative philosophy.

"Now," says the Apostle Paul, "I want you to understand something. When you became a steward of the mysteries, you became a recipient of revealed theology. God leaned out of heaven and told you about Himself. Then He told you about yourself and made sense of life as He revealed the truth to you. And remember," Paul says, "it wasn't just for you. He entrusted this information to you in order that those around you whose eyes are blinded by the god of this world might, through you, have their eyes opened."

What a sense of privilege! And you get excited, you feel something welling up inside you, and you say, "I've got my little oar, and I've got my dose of revelation, and I'm here to pull on my little oar, and I'm here to be a trustworthy steward, a noble trustee of all this information. God, I want to be faithful."

A MATTER OF PRIDE

Faithfulness, of course, is the next step. Paul says, "Now it is required that those who have been given a trust must prove faithful" (1 Corinthians 4:2). Why would they want to be faithful? Because they have such a sense of pride in their privileged position that they say in effect, "Fancy God calling me. Fancy God choosing me. Fancy God deciding to do it this way. Fancy me getting in on it. It's wonderful. It's thrilling." And they reason from there, "Lord, I don't want to blow it; I don't want to fall on my nose. I want to be faithful to that to which You have called me. I can't believe that You trusted me, but You did, and I'm going to respond." Therein lies the sense of privilege, and it is entirely appropriate to be proud of such privilege.

Assuming you are a Christian, what is it that motivates *you* in *your* Christian life? We've discussed several motivational factors thus far in this book. Sometimes when we don't find ourselves responsive to one, we need to find ourselves responsive to another. Perhaps as you are reading this, some of you are saying, "I've lost my sense of privilege. I've lost that sense of pride in being called by the Lord Jesus and entrusted by Him, and, as a result of that, I've been very slack. I've been spiritually sloppy. I've been motivated by other considerations. Lord, forgive me."

THE MATTER OF PRESSURE

What makes it difficult for us to fulfill the sense of privilege bestowed upon us by God? Pressure. And the Apostle Paul's next words to the believers of Corinth are about the pressures to which he is subjected. He doesn't state them overtly, but they are certainly there. Look at 1 Corinthians 4:3: "I care very little if I'm judged by you or by any human court; indeed, I do not even judge myself." Three kinds of pressure are involved here. First of all, the pressure exerted on Paul by the Corinthian church. Second, the pressure exerted on him by what he calls the human court. And third, the pressure that he exerts on himself.

When we endeavor to be faithful and sometimes find ourselves slacking off, the reason may be that we have been subjected to pressures that have become more influential than our sense of privilege. If that is the case, we need to identify those pressure points.

The first one we'll identify as pressure from the Christian community of which Paul was a part, because He says to the Corinthians, "I am being judged by you." And of course, he was. He was subjected to the same kinds of pressure points that all Christians are subjected to in Christian communities. Let me mention a few of them.

The pressure of manipulation. Most people are very comfortable with the status quo, because they've worked hard to make the status exceedingly quo, and they don't want it un-quoing. Now then, somebody new comes in. He's all bright-eyed and bushy-tailed and has his oar well-oiled and is pulling diligently on it, and several fellow believers tap him on the shoulder and say, "Hold it. That is not necessary around here. We have never done it that way before." And then they begin to pull from the files pages and pages of material. They take out constitutions. They show policies. They begin to effectively lock this newcomer in, to manipulate him, thus ensuring that absolutely nothing is changed. Everyone who's ever been involved in Christian work anywhere at any time sooner or later has come up with that kind of hand-tying situation.

A senior pastor in Minnesota once told me that one of his gravest concerns about the ministry is the tremendous number of young pastors who are quitting. And he said more often than not they are giving up because they have found it impossible to exercise any leadership whatsoever in the congregation. What he was really saying is that they come out of their training with a high sense of calling. They're bright-eyed and bushy-tailed at first, but as they keep butting their heads against a brick wall, they soon find that their hands are tied and their sense of privilege in serving the Lord has been lost.

The pressure of adulation. This is the pressure that comes from people who think you're absolutely marvelous. They won't hear a word said against you. An example from my own experience will well illustrate this. A widow used to live a few doors away from us, and early one morning as I was driving past her home, I saw her shoveling snow off her drive, so I stopped and said, "Let me help you."

"Don't waste your time doing that," she replied. "You get out there and tell 'em. In fact, I was trying to get my driveway cleared so I could get a start on yours. You know that my husband and I went to church all our lives. We never knew that we could give our lives to Jesus until one Sunday when we visited your church. We only came one time, but we both got saved the first time we ever walked in. And you remember a few days later my husband died and you buried him? Well, I know he's in heaven, and if you hadn't been there telling us and if there hadn't been that place there for us to be told, what on earth would have happened to us? Don't waste your time shoveling drives. You just get out there. Go and tell 'em." And then she added, "By the way, I heard that there were some people in that church who were giving you a hard time."

"Did you hear that?"

"Yes, I heard that. Listen. If any more of those people ever give you a hard time, send them to me." And immediately I could see a list of people that I would like to send! Particularly because, as she said it, she was enforcing her point by waving her snow shovel in the air!

We can all take that kind of adulation, can't we? The trouble with praise is that it puts another type of pressure on you. You try to avoid the manipulators; the adulators, on the other hand, are a tempting bunch to spend all your time with. Unfortunately, they're both exerting pressure on you and both can take you away from being fundamentally faithful out of a sense of privilege. Therein lies the problem.

The pressure of confrontation. Do you ever find yourself in a community of believers where you seem to be continually having a confrontation? Some people are just natural opposers. I don't know why, but they are. I've often observed that most churches have a little group of these supersaints. They preface everything they say with, "The Lord told me." Sometimes these supersaints come to counsel me because they can see that I'm clearly not in their category. They talk to me about what the Lord said to them, and then they do a strange thing. They ask, "What do you think?"

How do you respond to people like that? I've tried various approaches. I've said, "Well, if He says it, I'm agin' it." They didn't like that. I was being facetious, of course. I've tried, "Funny He should have told you, because I was just talking to Him a minute ago, and He never said a word to me about it." That doesn't work either.

Confrontational people who've got a special "in" with the Lord assume that very few other people around them have it. They very rarely flex, very rarely adjust. And absolutely nobody can handle them for the very simple reason that the Lord hasn't told anybody else what He told them, and there's absolutely no way of checking on it!

We had a group of supersaints in our church years ago. I could recognize them from the pulpit. They would sit in the pews looking as if they'd been sucking lemon drops and had acquired acidosis. I would say something during the sermon and their pained expressions would become excruciating and their heads would bow in prayer. The question I kept asking was, "Lord, what are they praying?" Well, I found out one day.

Unknown to me, another portion of the congregation went to talk to the holier-than-thous and said, "Listen, why don't you get excited about the Lord Jesus and get into things and be part of the fellowship and share in what God is doing?"

And the supersaints answered, "Because the Lord said . . ." and they told them what the Lord had said.

"Well, listen, if the Lord's saying all that to you, why don't you get out of this apostate place?"

"Because the Lord has told us to stay here and pray Briscoe out."

Now, that's encouraging, isn't it? That's the pressure that can break your heart!

Let's always remember that we need to identify the pressure points that come from within the Christian community, because sometimes they can be so powerful they become more important to us than being what the Lord called us to be. From my personal perspective, I would have to say that the varied pressures of manipulation, adulation, and confrontation can respectively tie your hands, swell your head, and break your heart. When that happens the strain can be practically unbearable, and great care is needed to maintain a proper outlook. And that is not all!

There's another kind of pressure—that which comes from the "human court." In the Greek the words literally mean "man's day." *Man*, as opposed to God, relates to the secular as opposed to the spiritual. And *day* here refers to that which is contemporary. So I think that what Paul is talking about is the kind of pressure exerted not from the congregation, but from external sources in Corinth, external sources in Ephesus, external sources in contemporary, secular society.

Some Christians never have to bother about this tension at all. They have decided that their Christianity should be lived in a tight little cocoon. This cocoon serves to isolate and insulate them from the nasty society outside, and permits them to have little or no realistic contact with it. They do not see themselves in any shape or form pulling on an oar into secular society to get Jesus there. They do not see themselves in any shape or form moving into secular society as stewards of the mysteries. I don't believe the Lord Jesus ever gave His church the freedom to do that. I believe that the church of Jesus Christ is called to be moving into man's day, moving out into the secular world and impacting it for God.

As we begin to move into situations of identifying with this society, that in itself will put us under pressure. Some people, for instance, feel very strongly about the abortion issue and refuse to sit idly by as 1.5 million babies each year are killed before they are born. So they move into secular society because they recognize that is where the decisions are being made; that is where the action is. And as they make inroads into the moral battle, they find themselves under new and special pressures. They find themselves caught up in the political machinery, and if they're not careful, they can simply become cogs in a wheel. Eventually they ask themselves, "How on earth did I get myself here?" While pulling on an oar to get Jesus into secular society, they got themselves so pressurized they forgot why they entered the fight in the first place.

Other believers say, "We have to do something about the nuclear buildup. We must, in the name of Christ, be peacemakers in our world." If they're determined to tackle the arms issue, they find that they must move into the corridors of power, and as they move into the corridors of power, they discover that they are subjected to all kinds of secular, contemporary pressure. And if they're not careful, they may find themselves caught up with the strangest theological, political, and ethical bedfellows they could ever imagine. And then they will sit down one day and wonder, "How did I ever get myself into this predicament?"

What an exciting thing to be light in the midst of darkness, to be salt in the midst of corruption, to be a child of God in our world today. But while enjoying the privilege, we must beware the pressures that come from outside sources.

There's a third pressure which the Apostle Paul mentions—that which he puts on himself.

I always remember an old pastor friend advising me, "There are two approaches you can take to the pastorate, Stuart. You can be as idle as the day is long and get away with it, because the people you are accountable to are all businessmen. All you need to do when they try to evaluate things their way is come up with theological answers to practical questions. That's how the churches of our land got full of pastors who aren't worth their salt. The other alternative is to go into the pastorate and send yourself to an early grave by assuming that you alone carry the weight of the burden of that church, and you alone are responsible for turning that city around for God. You're not very smart if you take either tack."

Some people, quite frankly, put no pressure on themselves at all. Other people put such excruciating pressure on themselves that they try to live up to their own unrealistic expectations. They expect of themselves only success, always victory. They expect of themselves continual, visible, tangible growth. They expect perfection. To put themselves under that kind of pressure means that inevitably they will forget why God put them here, because their criteria have nothing to do with what Jesus wants.

A MATTER OF PERSPECTIVE

If you find yourself under self-imposed pressure; if you find yourself under pressure from secular society; if you find yourself under pressure in the Christian community, what happens? Did you ever see the circus performer who comes out with a whole pile of plates and sticks some canes in the ground or in a stand? He puts a plate on the top of one cane, starts spinning it, and keeps it going, then grabs another plate and gets it going. Soon you realize he's not just doing three, but six, twelve, fifteen, and in the end he's whirling from one end to the other and the plates are wobbling, and he gives them a twist and he's going around and . . . did you ever feel like that? Did you ever feel you were trying to keep fifteen plates spinning all at once?

There's one overriding thought you need to keep in mind when you get yourself in a situation like that: "I am privileged to be a servant of Christ. I am privileged to be a steward of the mysteries, and there's only one thing I must do—be faithful."

Notice that the Apostle Paul handles all these vise grips in a very unusual way. He simply nullifies the pressure points. "I care very little if I am judged by you," he says (1 Corinthians 4:3).

I can see Paul's amanuensis (secretary) at that moment looking up and saying, "You want me to write that?"

"Yes."

"You don't mean that?"

"Yes."

"You mean you're going to tell those Corinthians, 'I care very little if I am judged by you'?"

"Yes."

"Well, that'll go over like a lead balloon down in Corinth."

"I know. But it's the truth. Oh, by the way, while you're at it, tell them I care very little if I'm judged by any human court either. Indeed, I do not even judge myself."

(What the Apostle Paul is saying in essence is this: "Look, you're sure to be subjected to a whole list of pressures and you've got to discount most of them.")

And so, the secretary looks up and says to Paul, "You are an anarchist. You are lawless. You're just doing your own thing, man."

Paul says, "No, I'm not through yet. Just write this down: 'There is One who judges me, and that is the Lord.'"

And the secretary writes it down and says, "Oh, wow!"

Think about this in personal terms for a minute. It's just possible that you've been spinning your plates to keep the Christian community happy. Perhaps you've been spinning your plates over the years to keep secular society off your back. And maybe you've been spinning those plates to help you fulfill your own unrealistic expectations. But the one thing you forgot is the one thing you should have remembered: it is the Lord who judges you and, therefore, you'd better get things into perspective.

Paul does this very thing, for underlying his statement is this line of thought: "It was the Lord who called me to be His servant; it was the Lord who called me to be His steward. It was the Lord who equipped me; it was the Lord who gave me this high privilege; and it is to Him that I'm answerable." (When you think about it, that is pressure enough.)

Just a word of warning in closing. The Apostle Paul is *not* saying here, "Nobody's going to tell me what to do." For he himself in this same epistle talks about the body of Christ, its members, and how they need one another. We need to be careful not to take this verse out of its context, but to understand the thrust.

PERSONAL REFLECTION

Dear Father, I realize how easy it is to lose my sense of privilege and to succumb to the most demanding pressures. I recognize how readily I can lose my sense of perspective and forget that while I am trying to keep everybody happy and off my back I need to be primarily concerned about being faithful to You and ultimately accountable to You. Such a truth is liberating to me because it frees me from the fear and tyranny of man, machine, and manipulative forces, and places me under Your gracious, firm control. Thank You, Lord!

"I thank my God every time I remember you. In all my prayers for all of you, I always pray with joy because of your partnership in the Gospel from the first day until now, being confident of this, that He who began a good work in you will carry it on to completion until the day of Christ Jesus.

"It is right for me to feel this way about all of you, since I have you in my heart; for whether I am in chains or defending and confirming the Gospel, all of you share in God's grace with me. God can testify how I long for all of you with the affection of Christ Jesus."

PHILIPPIANS 1:3-8

five
MOVED BY COMPASSION

Peter Ustinov, the actor, playwright, director, raconteur, linguist, and humorist, is one of the funniest, brightest men that I've ever had the opportunity of reading or watching. He has a keen eye, loves to observe human foibles, and has a sardonic wit. He sees what is going on in society and is able to poke fun at it, making people laugh at their own inconsistencies.

One of the things Ustinov said recently was full of his typical observation and wit. "Charity," he said, "is more common than compassion, because charity is tax deductible while compassion is merely time-consuming." There's something humorous about that. But there's also something cutting and terribly compelling about it, because he's absolutely right.

We're grateful for the fact that we live in a nation where it is possible to get tax deductible receipts for our charity. Frankly, I know of no other nation on the face of God's earth where citizens have that privilege. But there's a danger to such a luxury. It allows us to do something about needs, but to do it at arm's length. It allows us to do something for others, but at the same time to feel satisfaction because we're gaining something for ourselves. There's all the difference in the world between cold charity and warmhearted compassion. Charity can be purely external, coldly calculated. But compassion is internal, a motivation of the heart that is pure, rich, and absolutely vital. It is also a distinctive motivational factor as far as spiritual experience is concerned.

THE COMPASSION OF GOD

When we think of compassion, we need to ask ourselves: where does it originate? And the answer is that compassion flows from the very heart of God.

So rich is this concept of compassion in the Scriptures that a whole fistful of Greek words are used to describe it, and more than one Hebrew word as well. English equivalents include: to love; to pity; to show mercy; and to suffer alongside of. Another translation is very common, though seemingly out of place among the likes of love and pity, mercy and suffering. It is the expression *gut feeling*.

The Greeks believed that the intestines, the internal organs, were the seat of the emotions. When they talked about compassion, they believed it was such a deeply felt emotion that the inner organs were literally tied up in a knot. This is the word Paul uses when he tells the believers of Philippi, "I long for all of you with the affection of Christ Jesus" (Philippians 1:8). It means "an utter gut-wrenching feeling; to be in an absolute knot inside." The sheer force of the word is evident when we realize that it is also used to describe God's attitude toward us. God, in an anthropomorphic sense, has a gut-wrenching concern for His people.

Let's review some Old Testament history. When God called His covenant people to Himself, beginning with Abraham, He did so out of concern for them. As time went by, these Hebrews found themselves in Egypt, captives of a merciless regime. They were having the most awful time, were desperately abused, and they cried to the Lord for help. Then one day, God spoke to Moses and said, "I have heard the cry of My people and have been moved with compassion for them. I am going to do something about it by sending you to be their deliverer" (see Exodus 3:7-10). Now notice that the motivation behind all this was God's sense of pity, His desire to show mercy, His gut-wrenching compassion toward His suffering people. So Moses went to Egypt and became the human means of the Children of Israel's deliverance from the land.

After escaping from the Pharaoh and crossing the Red Sea, this wandering tribe of 2 million-plus finally arrived in the wilderness where the people suddenly forgot years of oppression and became homesick for Egypt. Moses had a terrible time with these complaining, stiff-necked folk. He worked with them, scolded them, tried all kinds of approaches. Eventually, he decided he'd had it with the whole lot, so he got up and preached a sermon which started with the immortal words, "Hear me, you rebels!"

At that point God decided it was about time He took Moses to one side for a refresher course, but not in public relations, or homiletics, or even hermeneutics. The refresher course was in God Himself. The Lord said to Moses, "I'm going to show you one more time what I'm like." And so, in Exodus 34, we have that gorgeous autobiographical passage where God speaks about Himself. Reading this passage carefully, we see the dominant theme is that God is a God of mercy, a God who shows pity, a God of compassion.

As time went on, God continued to deal with His people, the nation Israel. Over and over He sent prophets to remind them that their behavior was unacceptable and to motivate them to come back to Him. Over and over the prophets declared that God had shown Israel His mercy, had pitied their estate, had loved them, had suffered with them, had stuck with them through all their trials. Jeremiah recalled that God's compassions are new every morning, that His faithfulness never changes (Lamentations 3:23). (That of course is the passage from which we get our favorite hymn, "Great Is Thy Faithfulness.") But he also recalled that if it were not for God's compassion, they would all have been "consumed" (3:22). In other words, the prophet reminded the Children of Israel that there was only one reason they continued to exist. There was only one reason they had been redeemed. And that was because of the compassion, the mercy, the generosity, the gut-wrenching willingness to suffer with His people that God had exhibited.

This is the basis from which we as believers today move. This is where compassion originates. God reveals to us what compassion is all about.

THE COMPASSION OF GOD MADE FLESH

But we human beings feel that we need a clearer demonstration of compassion. God is too remote. The history of Israel is too theological, too historical. Knowing this, God sent His Son, who laid aside His glory, assumed our humanity, was born in our likeness, and lived among us. And as He lived among us, he modeled compassion.

On one occasion, Jesus saw the people wandering aimlessly like sheep without a shepherd. He knew that their society was disintegrating. He saw that they were physically hungry and that many were sick among them. What was His reaction? He was moved with compassion, and here again the Gospel writer uses that Greek word meaning "gut-wrenching." Our Lord Jesus began to reach out to people. He healed the ill, fed the hungry, redeemed the lost. He spoke to their broken society. He gave of Himself to them. He became compassion in action.

Having modeled it for them, Jesus then gathered His disciples around Him and repeatedly taught them about compassion. One such lesson was the Parable of the Unmerciful Servant, recorded in Matthew 18. The story is of a man who owed his superior a lot of money, but didn't have the funds to repay the debt. So he fell down before his superior and begged for compassion. And the superior mercifully forgave him and wiped the ledger clean. Relieved of the heavy debt, the forgiven man left the house and promptly bumped into his friend, whom he grabbed by the throat and demanded, "Pay me what you owe me." Even though he had been forgiven a debt 64,000 times greater, he himself was unwilling to forgive. And the Lord Jesus said in effect, "That is totally unacceptable behavior. Those who have benefited from the compassion of God ought to begin to discover a compassionate spirit within themselves."

The Apostle Paul picks up this same theme in the Book of Romans. After writing eleven chapters of solid theology outlining God's compassionate mercy and grace, he says, "I beseech you therefore, brethren, by the mercies [the compassions] of God, that you present your bodies a living sacrifice" (Romans 12:1, NKJV). Paul's point is simply this: "If you understand the compassionate mercy of God in your own life, that in itself is motive enough to bring you to a point of utter dedication to the Lord."

The compassion of God . . . it is the very basis of our existence, our redemption, our survival. Understanding this, we should look into our own hearts and see whether something of that nature has been imparted to us by the Holy Spirit. Put in the simplest terms: if I have tasted compassion, am I disseminating it?

GENERATING COMPASSION

Understanding God's compassion and realizing we ought to be motivated by it to express compassion to others is only the first step in the process. There are roadblocks.

Some Christians reason, "I know all about compassion and I know it's right, but it really bothers me. I don't like being ripped off. This world is full of rogues, and I feel that if I start being compassionate, they're going to take me to the cleaners." Others contend, "I've found if you start being compassionate and soft with people, you'll end up a doormat. And I don't think you achieve anything by being a doormat." Still others argue, "I know people out there are in need, but the reason they're in need is that they're lazy. In this great country of ours, in this land of opportunity, if people have needs it's their own fault. To give them a handout is the worst possible thing you can do."

But all the arguments fail to erase the fact that Jesus said quite simply and categorically: "If you have been shown compassion (and God certainly has shown it to you), then you need to show it too." But how, especially if we have inner feelings to the contrary? Let's look at Psalm 14, because I believe that will give us the answer to our question.

> The fool says in his heart, "There is no God."
> They are corrupt, their deeds are vile;
> There is no one who does good.
> The Lord looks down from heaven on the sons of men
> To see if there are any who understand,
>   any who seek God.
> All have turned aside, they have together
>   become corrupt;
> There is no one who does good, not even one.
> Will evildoers never learn—
> Those who devour My people as men eat bread
> And who do not call on the Lord?
> There they are, overwhelmed with dread,
> For God is present in the company of the righteous.
> You evildoers frustrate the plans of the poor,
> But the Lord is their refuge.
> Oh, that salvation for Israel would come out of Zion!
> When the Lord restores the fortune of His people,
> Let Jacob rejoice and Israel be glad!

I included the complete psalm to get to what I feel is the most important word, located in the last verse and containing only two letters: *Oh*. It is the crux of this psalm and the shortest text I have ever taught in my life.

Notice that you can say *Oh* in a variety of ways: as an

exclamation; as a mere statement; even with a touch of surprise. Or you can read it the way the psalmist intended it to be read and say, "oooooHHHHH!" conveying the deep, gut-wrenching concern present in the heart of God.

Psalm 14 illustrates that compassion is generated in two ways. First of all, by understanding the *human condition*, and then, secondly, by recognizing the *human potential.*

Let's start with the human condition and David's words, "The fool says in his heart, 'There is no God' " (Psalm 14:1). The word *fool* can mean many things in contemporary English. It may refer to someone who puts paint on his face, dresses up in a funny costume, and cavorts about a circus tent. Or, it could be a half-wit or a dimwit—someone who doesn't really have his act together. It can be a person who is a bit of a comedian, or someone who is very superficial and resists getting serious. But here it doesn't mean any of those things. *Fool* in the Old Testament means someone who refuses to respond to God's revelation of Himself. The biblical fool has adopted a hard attitude and clings to a determined, anti-God position.

We've all met these people. We may even have some in our churches. I don't say this in an insulting way. There are foolish people in the divine economy who are very, very intelligent indeed. In fact, sometimes their intelligence has become a trap. They may be geniuses in physics. They can manipulate computers. They can figure out how to get a man on the moon, and, more importantly, how to get him back again. They can look at microbiological things and understand them. They can grapple with human need, get into the intricacies of human emotions, and unravel the mysteries of the human brain. They can do mathematical equations beyond imagination. Their problem is that they're so brilliant that they think they can figure out everything, and because they can't figure out God, they've decided He's not there.

Others who fall into the category of biblical foolishness are very sensitive individuals, far more sensitive than many

Christians. They have looked around the world and have been absolutely heartbroken by what they have seen. And sometimes their very sensitivity to human need has militated against them accepting the notion of God, for they reason, "If there were a God, something would have been done about this."

What's interesting about the first sentence of Psalm 14 is that it could equally be translated, "The fool says in his heart, 'No, God.' " In other words, the fool believes that God is, but he also believes that he can say no to Him and get away with it. So he spends all his time fighting with a God he's trying terribly hard to prove isn't there in the first place!

When we see people tying themselves into such knots, do we react with disinterest or contempt, merely writing them off? We shouldn't, for that too is hardness of heart. We need to say, "ooooohhhhh," with the intensity and feeling of the psalmist. An understanding of the human condition helps us begin to generate genuine concern within our hearts.

David next writes about the fallenness of man: "They are corrupt, their deeds are vile; there is no one who does good. The Lord looks down from heaven on the sons of men to see if there are any who understand, any who seek God. All have turned aside, they have together become corrupt" (Psalm 14:1-3). How can we explain the way the human race behaves? I believe the biblical explanation is the only one that gets even close to making sense. The Bible says man was created in the image of God and given fantastic capabilities by the Creator. But it also says that man is fallen. So as we look at humanity not only do we see vestiges of the image of God as demonstrated by God-given creativity and ingenuity, but mingled with it everything that is so bad and contrary to all God is.

I was thinking about this one day many years ago while aboard a thirteen and a half-hour, nonstop flight from London to Los Angeles. As we flew over the North Pole, the clouds parted and I looked down to see Greenland. (Why they call it Greenland, I don't know. It isn't.) Viewing that expanse of nothingness I thought, "What a disaster! Man hasn't been here. It's just barren, cold wilderness, howling gales and snowdrifts, ice and polar bears. Who'd want to live there?" Fortunately, as we headed south, I began to see the ice caps give way to the tundra. And I saw a straight line and realized man had been there. That straight line went to a little village, and then from the village, two straight lines, two villages, and then a network, and eventually we reached the prairies. Here I saw the fantastic work that man has done and felt pride in knowing we can produce enough food to feed millions of people. We traveled farther south and I began to see the vineyards, the arable areas, the livestock. Then the towns and the cities, the freeways and the automobiles. Next came the great metropolis of San Francisco and finally Los Angeles from the air. By this time I was high just thinking about being a human being!

As we landed and somebody opened the door, the smog came rolling in. My throat began to tingle, my eyes began to water, and everyone started jostling to get off the airplane. I began to sour a little bit on the human race. Then we entered customs, and the souring effect intensified. The next hassle was the baggage claim area, where people were getting bags mixed up and arguing with each other. Eventually I retrieved my luggage and came out to meet my friends. The first thing they said to me was, "Hurry, you've got a meeting in an hour," after which they hustled me into their car and sped onto the freeway. Within five minutes we were in a twelve-car accident complete with tires screeching, glass shattering, and sirens blowing. And I thought, "I've had it with the human race! I don't want to belong to it! Make me something else, God."

If we truly want to understand the human race, we have some serious thinking to do: "How do I account for man's creativity? How do I account for his ingenuity? How do I account for the remarkable things that he does? And on the other side, how do I account for the fact that every time man creates, he destroys? How do I account for the fact that every time man initiates, he initiates something good *and* something bad? And how do I account for the fact that man is capable of so much richness, yet so much poverty; so much beauty, yet so much ugliness? There's only one way I can—by realizing that mankind is fallen." People who try to tell us that man is slowly, inexorably improving are denying the evidence.

But when we think of the fallenness of man, how do we react? With indifference? With disgust? Or with that gut-wrenching sigh of the psalmist? "If this is what man can do in his fallen state, *oh*, to see him restored to a right relationship with the God who made him. *Oh*, if we could only cultivate the glimmering vestiges of the image of God in him. *Oh*, if we could eliminate this dark side of his character and see him freed to become in truth a child of God."

First, foolishness. Then, fallenness. As David continues this psalm, he examines man's filthiness. He talks about the evildoers who never learn, who frustrate the plans of the poor, and about the corruption that abounds.

Let's face it. Sometimes it is a nasty business to live among human beings. I was reminded of this some time ago when I conducted a wedding at our church. At the end of the ceremony, I went out into the foyer, waiting while everyone worked their way through the reception line. As I waited, I saw a couple crying quietly in the corner. It had been a rather emotional wedding, but I wasn't quite sure why they were crying, so I went over and asked, "What's the problem?"

The lady said, "Oh, I'm just absolutely torn up inside. For four years I battled a divorce suit my husband served me. There were absolutely no grounds for it and I didn't want it. And here I was at this beautiful wedding, reminded again of what God says about marriage. It was all so beautiful and so lovely, yet my divorce was finalized just this week. The thing that really got to me was that the man sitting in front of me was the judge who declared my marriage null and void. I'm sorry—I feel I can't take it any longer."

Then I turned my attention to the young fellow about half her age crying with her. I thought, "What a delightful thing, seeing a young man so concerned." Then she said, "His problem is far worse than mine."

And the man told this story: "My brother and I serve together as paramedics. Yesterday we were called out on an emergency. As we reached the general area of the call, we were given the address, which turned out to be the home of our parents. When we arrived, we found one of our brothers lying dead with a bullet through his head and our other brother sitting in the chair holding the gun with which he'd just committed the murder."

That's our church, folks. Upper middle-class suburbia.

What is it about man that causes him to shoot his brother and divorce his wife? What causes him to spend his greatest resources on armaments, and yet ignore the hungry, homeless, and hurting? There's something basically wrong with us, something messy, something filthy. Yet what do we do about it? We study the statistics, list the offenses, and utter a polite, "Oh."

Perhaps the time has come for us to have that gut-wrenching feeling that God has, to begin to look at the foolishness of man, the fallenness of man, the utter filthiness of man and say, "OOOOOHHHHH! Oh, that God might move again in our world!" For when we grasp God's compassionate nature and begin to be moved by it, then we will become properly motivated Christians, revealing the heart of God to our world.

While thus far I have concentrated on the negative aspect of man, I also want to recognize the great wealth of human potential. Look at what David says next: "God is present in the company of the righteous" (Psalm 14:5). What does that tell us but that man was created in such a way that he is capable of being a divine residence. Or, to put it in the simplest possible terms: man, in all his need, can actually help God come and dwell in the very center of his life. The

God of grace, the God of mercy, the God of peace, the God
of love, the God of justice can enter amidst the horror, the
dirtiness, the unkindness of our race and of our lives. He
can actually come inside and clean us up, cause us to do a
180-degree revolution. Realizing this, we should ask ourselves, "Why is it that when we know what man could be,
when we know what God longs to do, that so little is
happening? ooooohhhhh!" This too is compassion.

Not only that, the psalmist goes on to say that God is a
refuge for the poor (14:6). People are poor in many senses:
financially, intellectually, morally, sociologically. It is so
easy for us to look at them and say, "Oh." But the Lord
doesn't do that. He is committed to being a refuge for the
poor, opening His arms wide to those who have needs of
any kind.

When we consider the plight of the hungry, there is
absolutely no reason on the face of God's earth that those
people should be suffering famine because He has already
provided for them. It isn't that there isn't enough food for
them; it's that the food isn't getting to them. And why not?
Because of fallen man, that's why. When we consider the
fate of unwanted fetuses, it isn't that there aren't enough
loving people to care for newborn babies; it isn't that there
aren't enough opportunities for them to grow up to lead
robust, healthy lives; it isn't that God wouldn't wonderfully
welcome them into His presence. The problem is that fallen
man has interrupted God's plans. God is a refuge. God has
what it takes. But man often throws a wrench in the divine
workings. When we truly recognize this, we say to ourselves, "You know, God could be working in people's lives.
There's so much that He would love to do. There's so much
that He's committed to doing. Oh. ooooohhhhh."

So we see compassion generated as we understand the
human condition; we see it generated as we recognize the
human potential. But how is it going to work out in our
lives? The answer is twofold. Compassion comes initially by
an emotional response, then by commitment to activity.

Peter Ustinov's words bear repeating at this point: "Charity is more common than compassion, because charity is tax deductible while compassion is merely time-consuming." Compassion is going to happen only when we get around to allowing some of our time, energy, and resources to be consumed by people in need.

Let me retell our Lord Jesus' brief but beautiful Parable of the Good Samaritan. A certain man went from Jerusalem to Jericho and fell among thieves. They took his money, stripped him, and left him beaten in a ditch, half-dead. By chance a priest came along. He looked at the wounded traveler and said, "Oh." And by chance a Levite came that way. He looked at the wounded traveler and said, "Oh," making a note to refer it to a committee who would appoint a subcommittee to look into ways of dealing with the mishap. And at last a Samaritan passed by, saw the tragic situation, and cried, "ooooOHHHHH!" He climbed off his donkey, got down in the muck and the nettles (ripping his own clothes in the process), poured oil and wine on the man's wounds and bound them up. All the while he was in robber-infested country, knowing that at any moment he too could be clubbed on the back of the head. He picked the man up, put him on his donkey, took him to an inn, paid for the room, and promised to return. That's compassion. Not just a warm feeling. Not just a bleeding heart. Not just liberal tendencies. Not just giving hand-outs. Compassion is *action* motivated by the understanding that God's concern for me is the sole reason I exist and survive. Therefore, I want to show compassion to people around me and give of myself to them. Motivated by God's compassion on my behalf, I long to meet others at their point of need, in Jesus' name. I want to be the means of an answer.

Powerful things will begin to happen in our lives as we allow our hearts to be touched by the Spirit. We will begin to understand human need, human condition, and human potential, and we will say, "Lord, I'd like very much to be part of the answer rather than exacerbating the problem. I'd like You to do something in me that will bring compassion to the surface so that I will actively involve myself, in Your name, to do what You would have me to do."

One of the great secrets of a vital fellowship with the Lord and with His church is a tremendous sense of compassion and concern. This chapter is intended to encourage those who already exhibit this godly motivation. But it's also intended to challenge those of us who perhaps haven't gotten around to understanding it yet. For those, my prayer is that you would ask God to make you sensitive to His compassion on your behalf and that you would then begin to exhibit the mind of Christ. Ask God to help you see the world as He sees it. And then ask Him to perform a divine heart transplant so you might honestly, genuinely be a person who has that gut-wrenching concern for those needy people around you, as you go to them in the name of Christ.

PERSONAL REFLECTION

Dear Father, I know that I can grow a shell around myself and live comfortably in it. It protects me from feeling what You feel and doing what You command. Thank You for cracking the shell. Now please, help me to grow out of it like a chicken leaving an egg, and help me take my first faltering steps into a world that has waited for me to be willing to be vulnerable.

"There are different kinds of gifts, but the same Spirit. There are different kinds of service, but the same Lord. There are different kinds of working, but the same God works all of them in all men.

"Now to each one the manifestation of the Spirit is given for the common good. To one there is given through the Spirit the message of wisdom, to another the message of knowledge by means of the same Spirit, to another faith by the same Spirit, to another gifts of healing by that one Spirit, to another miraculous powers, to another prophecy, to another the ability to distinguish between spirits, to another the ability to speak in different kinds of tongues, and to still another the interpretation of tongues. All these are the work of one and the same Spirit, and He gives them to each one, just as He determines.

"The body is a unit, though it is made up of many parts; and though all its parts are many, they form one body. So it is with Christ. For we were all baptized by one Spirit into one body—whether Jews or Greek, slave or free—and we were all given the one Spirit to drink."

1 CORINTHIANS 12:4-13

six
TEAM SPIRIT

Marcus Allen of the Los Angeles Raiders is regarded by those who understand American football as one of the greatest running backs of all time. But you would not always have known that. The first two years of his college career at the University of Southern California (USC) he simply blocked for fellow running back Charles White. And it must have been a very frustrating experience for him, with all the superlative gifts that he had, simply to charge into a defensive line and knock big men over so that another man could run through. Of course, after Charles White graduated, Marcus Allen came into his own and people began to see what he was really capable of doing. He won the Heisman Trophy his senior year, and now he's a professional athlete.

But why would a man of Allen's caliber be prepared to operate differently from what all his natural inclinations suggested he should? The answer is team spirit. He was not playing for Marcus Allen; he was playing for USC. He understood that, in that particular situation, his responsibility was to be of the greatest possible advantage to the team. It certainly was not going to win him the Heisman Trophy for individual collegiate excellence, but it was going to achieve a greater end, as far as he was concerned. It's amazing what team spirit will do in terms of motivation. It will get people to do what, individually, they would not be prepared to do.

The same thing happens in the military. When I joined the Marines, they sat us down and lectured us endlessly. The lectures were designed for people who normally didn't think and usually didn't read. We were simply presented the facts and required to memorize them. One of the expressions we had to memorize was *esprit de corps*. *Esprit de corps* means literally "spirit of a body." But to us Marines the idea was this: individual Marines can achieve certain things, but a regiment of Marines can accomplish the unimaginable.

This idea of team spirit, or *esprit de corps*, may sound strange when we think of the church of Jesus Christ, but, in fact, it is not strange at all. Actually, *esprit de corps* or body spirit is a term that fits very easily into theological thinking, because the Bible teaches that the church of Jesus Christ, the local fellowship of believers, is the body of Christ. Furthermore, people who are part of that body have a spirit, a motivating factor, they would otherwise not have. In other words, it is possible for Christians to operate Christianly on an individual basis, but they cannot operate fully on that basis. For if they do not understand the *esprit de corps*, the team spirit, that comes from being part of the body of Christ, they will be lacking in certain kinds of motivation.

With that in mind, then, let's talk about team spirit as a Christian motivating factor, including these three specifics: how to *generate* team spirit in the church, how to *demonstrate* team spirit in the church, and how to *perpetuate* team spirit in the church.

GENERATING TEAM SPIRIT

How do we generate team spirit in the church? First of all, by emphasizing our common experience. When believers get together in a discussion situation they tend to talk about things on which they differ. Such conversations are generally negative and not particularly productive. They can, in fact, be extremely destructive. Christians need to bear in mind that they have far more things in common than uncommon. They need to major on the majors.

An example of this commonality is that everyone who is truly a member of the body of Christ has had an experience of the living God that is very similar. Paul points out three such similarities in 1 Corinthians 12. First of all, he talks about the activity of God in people's lives (verse 6). In other words, if we have entered into a relationship with the Lord Jesus, it is because God took the initiative. God arrested our attention. God communicated something to us, touched our lives, and transformed them; He turned us around and set us off in a whole new direction. Now, that's a glorious concept! And it is a wonderful thing to realize this happened not only to you, but to all other believers.

Secondly, believers share in common the lordship of Christ. Paul writes that no one can say Jesus is Lord except by the Holy Spirit (verse 3), and that there are different ministries, but it is the same Lord overseeing them (verse 5).

When a lot of individuals do their individual things, friction and collisions are inevitable. If, however, those same individuals come under the common control (lordship) of Jesus Christ, one would expect those collisions to be minimized. Not eradicated, of course, because we don't always allow God to work in us as He would or acknowledge Christ as Lord as we should.

Thirdly, Paul mentions the common action of the Holy Spirit in our lives: there are different kinds of gifts but the *same* Spirit, who also enables each of us to acknowledge Jesus as Lord (verse 3). Clearly, we all experience the working of the Holy Spirit in our lives—convicting us of sin, convincing us of the truthfulness of Christ, converting us to a new lifestyle before the Lord Jesus. There is real oneness in Him.

In addition to concentrating on our common experiences, we can generate team spirit by emphasizing the common good. Paul says this very thing, "To each one the manifestation of the Spirit is given for the common good" (verse 7). This means that when I experience the working of God in my life, I must not assume that it is purely for my own consumption. God's activity in my life is also for the benefit of the body of believers to which I belong, with which I identify. Therefore I must be concerned not only with my individual condition and desires, but also for the condition and desires of the body as a whole.

This approach introduces a whole new factor into our thinking. It's easy for us to concentrate on individual desires and preferences. It's an entirely different thing, however, to realize that God is concerned for the common good, for the well-being and health of the entire body of believers. An interesting tension surfaces at this point because there's no question that this passage of Scripture also emphasizes the uniqueness of the individual.

For instance, in verse 13, Paul identifies the various backgrounds of those within the body at Corinth: some are Jews, some are Greeks, some are slaves, and some are free. We would put it differently in our own historical framework, but Paul is simply saying it would be ridiculous to suggest that we're all identical. We're not. We have come from widely differing circumstances.

Not only that, he points out that we have different callings. According to verse 18, "God has arranged the parts in the body, every one of them just as He wanted them to be." By that Paul means He has taken individual Christians from differing circumstances and has placed them in the body in different ways to do different things.

Moreover, he insists, we have individual capabilities. According to verse 11, the Holy Spirit works in our lives, giving different abilities to each person as He determines.

Having said all that, the Apostle Paul also says that despite our differences, we are interrelated in Christ. What's more, he says we are interdependent and illustrates this truth with the analogy of the human body. The members of the human body are very different for very obvious reasons, reminds Paul. None of them can say that the others are irrelevant or nonfunctional. Each part has its individual role to play, but the individual roles are inseparably woven, committed to the good, the health, the ongoing well-being of the body as a whole. Then Paul uses several humorous illustrations to drive home the point. "If the foot should say, 'Because I am not a hand, I do not belong to the body,' it would not for that reason cease to be part of the body. And if the ear should say, 'Because I am not an eye, I do not belong to the body,' it would not for that reason cease to be part of the body. If the whole body were an eye, where would the sense of hearing be? If the whole body were an ear, where would the sense of smell be?" (verses 15-17)

Imagine for a moment a little boy who is crying in Sunday School.

The teacher asks, "Why are you crying?"

"Because you just said God made me with my nose to smell and my feet to run."

"That's right."

"I think He made me all wrong, because it's my feet that smell and my nose that runs."

Just like this little chap who wasn't too sure about how each part should work, we sometimes feel at a loss to understand our function in the body of Christ. Suffice it to say that various members of the body, uniquely different, are all designed for the good of the body. And in the same way that the running back, for the good of the team, sometimes gives up the opportunity to carry the football in order that he might block for someone else, so we must sometimes submerge our individuality for the common good.

Another way we generate team spirit in the church is by emphasizing a common objective. The Apostle Paul finishes a sentence in 1 Corinthians 12:12 in a way that is very surprising indeed. He says: "The body is a unit, though it is made up of many parts; and though all its parts are many, they form one body. So it is with the church."

That's what we'd expect him to say—at least I would. But he doesn't. Instead he writes, "So it is with Christ." Does Paul mean that Christ is the church and the church is Christ? Of course not. What he is saying is that the church, in a very real sense, is an *extension* of Christ, His body. We'll see the significance of this in just a moment, but it is a truth that is sometimes overlooked. We have to recognize that in a very special way when believers identify with Christ, they must identify with each other. They must become a visible, tangible community because this is their calling as the body of Christ.

Let me illustrate further. When we were about to begin building our new church, the architect announced that he would like members of the congregation to give him their ideas of features to be incorporated. What an invitation! Unfortunately, when we added up the cost of all the wonderful ideas, it was in the neighborhood of $1.75 billion. So we decided to whittle things down a bit so that perhaps we could pay for the building in two or three lifetimes!

One of my suggestions to the architect was that we ought to have a gallery for the spirits.

And he said, "The what?"

"A gallery for the spirits."

"I don't understand," he replied, brows furrowed.

So I said, "Correct me if I'm wrong, but it seems that the main expense in building a building is the fact that people have bodies. For instance, you have told us how many square feet the state requires for each body. People also complain that it's too cold or it's too hot, so we have to keep the building heated or cooled to 70 degrees all the time. What's more, bodies need light and bodies need air. It seems to me that these bodies are very expensive."

"Well, I suppose so, if you put it that way," he admitted.

"That's why I would like us to have a gallery for the spirits, because every week people tell me, 'We're sorry we won't be able to be at church next Sunday, but we'll be with you in spirit.' So, why build square footage for spirits? Why heat a building for spirits? Why put in lighting if they don't need it?"

And he looked at me and said something less than enthusiastic about British humor.

Well, at least I enjoyed it! And I did have a point: we go anywhere we go because of our bodies, not because of our spirits. Our bodies can't do one thing and our spirits another. I'll concede that some of us sit in our bodies in church, but our spirits are on the eighth green. Or our bodies are in prayer meeting, but our minds are trying to remember if we turned off the oven. Yet I think we can all agree that the body is the means whereby the spiritual entity functions in a physical environment.

What then is the body of Christ? It is the corporate group of believers, consisting of all kinds of people, and united together to be the means whereby a spiritual Christ functions in a physical environment. The objective of the church, in short, is to make an invisible Christ visible, an intangible Christ tangible. We are here to be the mechanical means whereby the dynamic Christ touches people's lives.

There is no one human being who can actually fulfill this mandate because it requires diversity within unity that only the church universal can accomplish. And so we return to our question, "How do we generate team spirit in the church?" By emphasizing our common experience, the common good, and our common objectives. If we don't, we'll get off on all kinds of individual rabbit trails and we'll be a body in name only. But if we can agree on our commonality, we will find a whole new motivating factor: *esprit de corps.*

DEMONSTRATING TEAM SPIRIT

Once we begin to generate team spirit in a church, how do we demonstrate it? First of all, by showing the unity of the

Spirit. Let's review 1 Corinthians 12:4-6: "There are *different* kinds of gifts, but the *same* spirit. There are *different* kinds of service but the *same* Lord. There are *different* kinds of working, but the *same* God" (italics added). The Apostle Paul emphasizes here both differences and similarities, and in so doing he illustrates that which is wonderfully and beautifully unique about the body of believers. The unity of the church of Jesus Christ allows for all kinds of diversity, but the diversity in the church of Jesus Christ is never so diverse that it militates against a fundamental unity.

Our society is a diverse lot, but at times we have to draw the line. For instance, I've gone to the Performing Arts Center in Milwaukee to listen to the Milwaukee Symphony perform Beethoven's Ninth, which includes a great chorale arrangement in the last movement. All the members are beautifully clad in their black tuxedos or black gowns, and they all sing the same kind of stuff. Beethoven's stuff. But I find it hard to imagine a punker standing in the middle of the chorus sporting a spiked hairdo of violet, orange, and yellow and singing his own tune. The chorale has a fundamental unity which will not tolerate that kind of diversity.

Or take the English game of rugby, where a lot of big husky fellows who've nothing better to do with their boyish energies get together to beat up each other in the name of sport. I have yet to find women who have joined a rugby club in order that they might introduce flower arrangement or macramé. I know Rosey Grier does needlepoint, but that's the exception to the rule! These men wouldn't stand for it. They have a fundamental unity and they maintain that unity at the expense of diversity.

The difference between those kinds of organizations and the church of Jesus Christ, if I can stretch the analogy, is this: in the church of Jesus Christ there's room for the chorale *and* the punker. There's room for rugby *and* macramé. A fundamental unity exists that other groups don't have which will bind those people together. Therein lies the uniqueness of the Christian church, and we must insist on it, fight for it, and maintain it with all the energy we have. If we fail, we simply become a social club with vague spiritual connotations, and that is a counterfeit church. The true church of Jesus Christ demonstrates a unity that allows diversity.

The church also presents a diversity that protects all kinds of unity. Notice how Paul puts it. There's *one* Spirit at work, *one* Lord we acknowledge, *one* God in heaven. But having said that, Paul immediately reminds us that there are *different* gifts, *different* ministries, *different* ways of doing things.

If we ever get ourselves locked into a situation where we all have to be the same, there's only one thing we do, and only one way of doing it, we will destroy the beauty and the uniqueness of the body of believers. We will finish up with a body that's all eyes, all tongues, or all feet—and that is not a body; it's a monstrosity. The body of believers demonstrates a unique unity of the Spirit, a unity that requires all kinds of love and compassion, flexibility and openness. These are qualities we seldom find elsewhere, certainly not in the symphony chorale when the punker wants to join or on the rugby club when someone would rather arrange daisies.

I was trying to explain all this to a group of missionaries in Japan once—without any discernible effect. They were gazing out the window and actually I didn't blame them because the view was superb. We were up among the volcanoes, forests, and lakes of Hokkaido, and we had had far too many meetings already. So, since they weren't listening, I decided there was no point in me talking, and I stopped in midsentence. There was total silence for a minute before anyone noticed. And then, somebody leaned forward and asked, "Is anything wrong?"

I replied, "No, no. Why?" Then they all wanted me to say something. So I said, "Green." And I thought I ought to add to that, so I said, "Green green." By this time I had their total attention. They were on the edges of their seats.

"Come on, tell us more," they insisted.

Keeping them mystified, I announced, "We will now take a five-minute break. Go to the window, which is what you wanted to do anyway, and count the different shades of green." The missionaries all looked at me like I was crazy, but they did it.

When we reconvened, I asked a few questions. How many found more than thirty shades of green? They all had. How many of the greens clashed with other greens? None. How many of the greens were not greens? None. How many of the greens were more green than the other greens? None. In short, we discovered that when God made green, He made an innumerable diversity of greens, all of which had the unity of greenness.

Some of the group still didn't make the spiritual connection, so I tried again. "Look around at the noses in this room. Notice that when God made noses, He designed all of them to be between the eyes, below the hairline, if any, above the mouth, with two holes in the bottom. Yet everyone's nose is so different. That's because when God creates something, He creates a fundamental unity that allows for all kinds of diversity." At last, my audience understood.

Let's apply all of this to the church. God said, "I'm going to bring together the most diverse people imaginable. They will possess a fundamental unity, and I'm going to allow that unity to become something for which they will live and for which they would die if necessary. It will never, however, be a unity that possesses a dull uniformity. It will be a unity that allows for untold diversity." And so it is.

We also demonstrate team spirit through respect for the other members of the team. In 1 Corinthians 12:23 the Apostle Paul suggests that those less-visible members of our physical bodies may actually be more vital than the visible ones. Or, to put it another way, the less-noteworthy may in fact be more necessary. The body of believers works exactly the same way, says Paul.

While I was out of town one time, some folks asked me

about Jill and the kids. "Do you have pictures of them?" they inquired.

"Sure," I replied and brought out the photos.

"What a beautiful girl," they remarked about my daughter Judy.

"You're absolutely right," I agreed.

"What gorgeous eyes she has," they continued.

And I said, "You should see her intestines."

"Whatever do you mean?" they winced.

"Her intestines are terribly important," I explained, "because if they become blocked, those beautiful blue eyes will go crossed. There is a vital relationship between her intestines and her big, blue eyes."

My point, like Paul's, is this: some members of our bodies are not visible, yet they're extremely vital. The intestines and colon—who's going to talk about either in polite company? Instead we talk about hair and teeth and eyes. But what's the good of hair if the colon's cancerous? Or what's the good of eyes if the intestines are blocked?

Likewise, if we are going to be members of the body of Christ, we must realize that some members of the body will have more honor, more visibility, more respect. But it's just as important for the visible Christian to acknowledge, "There's a little person over there who's not visible, but he's absolutely vital." That's respect, and it is so delightfully beautiful when the body of Christ lives out this unity as it ought.

A third way we demonstrate our unity is by caring for the body as a whole. Paul writes, "There should be no division in the body, but . . . its parts should have equal concern for each other. If one part suffers, every part suffers with it; if one part is honored, every part rejoices with it" (1 Corinthians 12:25-26). In other words, members of the body of Christ ought to be characterized by care, not just for themselves, but for the body as a whole. We don't want the body divided. We don't want the body falling apart. We don't want any limbs amputated. We don't want certain parts giving other parts a hard time.

I once dealt with a situation where two groups of believers were quite upset with each other. In the end, one person said, "Don't you understand that we're just an arm of the church?" And when a member of the other faction didn't know how to answer, I said, "Yeah, he understands that. He just feels that the arm is sticking its finger in *his* eye."

We need to be concerned about the overall well-being of the body. And if we are, we must accept a fundamental truth: if one part of the body sins, it reflects on the body as a whole; or as Paul puts it, if one part suffers, the body suffers. By the same token, if one part of the body experiences God's blessing, the rest should feel perfectly free to bask in the warmth of that glory, because if part of the body is glorified, then all the members are glorified. If one member is honored, then it's an honor to the whole body.

PERPETUATING TEAM SPIRIT

Once we've generated team spirit and begun to demonstrate it, how do we maintain such unity in the church? The first and last verses of 1 Corinthians 12 give us two answers to this question.

First, Paul says, "I do not want you to be ignorant" (verse 1). We perpetuate team spirit in the church by waging war on ignorance. Many people are very ignorant about the "body of Christ" concept. Talk to them about the church and they immediately bring up denominations. Or buildings. Or they start comparing pastors. What on earth has any of that got to do with it? The church isn't somewhere we go. The church is something we are. *We* are the body of Christ!

Here's an enlightening experiment to try some time. Interview people coming out of church.

"Excuse me. Have you been to church?"

"Yes."

"What on earth were you doing?"

"Oh, the same thing I always do."

"Well, if you always do it, then presumably you know what you're doing."

"Yes."

"Well, what was it?"

Such is the sorry state of many Christians. They honestly don't know what the church is. Therefore, they honestly don't know what the church does. If we're going to perpetuate team spirit, we have to wage war against that kind of ignorance.

"Now," Paul says in conclusion, "I will show you the most excellent way" (verse 31). And with those words he introduces 1 Corinthians 13, the so-called love chapter. How else do we perpetuate team spirit in the church? By creating a loving, concerned atmosphere, by cultivating and demonstrating genuine interest in people. And we do it all out of love for Jesus Christ, so that His purposes might not be hindered.

Do you see how the body concept can spark powerful motivation? I can do my own thing and show up in church once in a while. Or I can decide I am going to do what I want to do no matter what the church feels about it. But neither of these approaches demonstrates team spirit. Team spirit enables me to feel caught up in something infinitely bigger than myself. Team spirit allows me to feel that I'm really contributing to what Jesus is doing in our world in this day and age. Team spirit makes me careful, because I realize that what I do doesn't just reflect on me, but on the body of Christ, and ultimately on Christ Himself.

PERSONAL REFLECTION

Thank God for the privilege and thrill of being a member of Christ's body, the church. Thank Him for allowing you to be what you never were before and to do what you never thought you could do—all because you are part of a wonderful unity of believers.

Perhaps this idea, this spiritual *esprit de corps*, is new to you. If so, ask God for a clear understanding of what He has for you in His body, the church. And there's no better way to do that than to become involved in a local fellowship. Or perhaps you understand the body concept, but find that your sense of team spirit has worn thin lately. If so, ask God to generate it afresh and enable you to demonstrate it in a lifestyle that brings great glory to Him and great blessing to the body of which you are a part.

"So we make it our goal to please Him, whether we are at home in the body or away from it. For we must all appear before the Judgment Seat of Christ, that each one may receive what is due him for the things done while in the body, whether good or bad. Since, then, we know what it is to fear the Lord, we try to persuade men."

2 CORINTHIANS 5:9-11

seven
THE FEAR
OF THE LORD

When A.W. Tozer, who pastored congregations in Toronto and Chicago for many years, died in 1963, one of the sharpest, most incisive Christian minds of recent years was silenced. Fortunately, Tozer left many of his thoughts for us in his writings. For instance, listen to these insightful words: "The history of mankind will probably show that no people has ever risen above its religion, and man's spiritual history will positively demonstrate that no religion has ever been greater than its idea of God" (*The Knowledge of the Holy,* Harper & Row, p. 7).

Tozer's point is well taken. No culture will develop purity, integrity, or justice to a degree higher than its religion. If its religion has little concept of justice, so will the culture. If its religion has little idea of purity and integrity, so will the culture. But then Tozer goes a step beyond secular matters to state that spiritual history will demonstrate that no religion has ever been greater than its idea of God. In other words, history is dependent on religion for quality and caliber, and the quality of any religion is dependent on that religion's concept of God. If there is a weak, inadequate concept of God, a weak, inadequate religion will result. If there is an erroneous concept of God, one can also expect an erroneous religion.

All societies tend to remake God in their own image, in *man's* image. For example, it is relatively easy for us to remake God in the image of the American Dream. We might even think we can substantiate this particular "doctrine" with passages of Scripture (of course, we would also have to carefully avoid others). But people in Third World countries would have trouble identifying with the American Dream and they would invent a God who would be very different indeed. They would, no doubt, find other passages of Scripture to make their God fit their culture.

We do not have the freedom to remake God after our culture. We are not at liberty to mold God to fit our preconceived ideas. God is immutable, unchanging. He has revealed Himself to us in His Word and if we are to live rightly on earth and to produce a righteous society around us, then we must first of all ensure that we are following that revelation accurately. If we do, we will begin to discover a tremendous response to the Lord.

As we have seen thus far in this book, if we concentrate on the grace of God, we will begin to generate the gratitude attitude. If we see God in Christ coming to serve us, then the servant spirit will come alive within us. If we recognize the love of God, then we will respond with concern and compassion. When we begin, however, to think in terms of God's holiness, righteousness, and justice, our response will be a tremendous sense of what the Bible calls repeatedly, "the fear of the Lord." If our attitude does not include a fear of the Lord, then it is because our understanding of God is inaccurate. That's why this motivational dynamic is so crucial.

WHAT DOES FEAR OF THE LORD MEAN?

What is meant by *the fear of the Lord?* First of all, an accurate understanding of truth. According to Proverbs 9:10, "The fear of the Lord is the beginning of wisdom, and the knowledge of the Holy One is understanding."

Notice two things here. If we are to have wisdom, if we're to build our understanding of life and reality on the proper base, the right attitude toward the Lord is fundamental. And the right attitude toward the Lord comes only from an accurate understanding of the Lord.

Each of us has favorite aspects of God's character, things He has done that are particularly appealing to us. But we don't have the freedom to pick just the ones we want. Our view of God must be complete. God is revealed in Scripture as the One who will be our final judge. He is revealed in Scripture as the One who acts in total righteousness, in absolute justice. He is described in Scripture as the One who is utterly pure and holy and who cannot tolerate sin. Any understanding of God that does not include these truths is inadequate. Any attitude toward God that does not respond to this sense of divine awesomeness must also be inadequate. Paul puts it this way: "We must all appear before the Judgment Seat of Christ, that each one may receive what is due him for the things done while in the body, whether good or bad" (2 Corinthians 5:10).

Of course, to balance this picture, we must remind ourselves that God is also a God of grace and that He is prepared to deal with us in a way that we don't deserve. When we acknowledge our sinfulness before His holiness, we qualify to receive His mercy and His grace. But for the purposes of this chapter, I want to focus on God's holiness, justice, and righteousness, and His capacity as judge. This will inevitably lead us to an accurate understanding of ourselves as well.

Second Corinthians 5:20-21 tells us that we need to be reconciled to God. That passage also tells us that God made Christ, who knew no sin, to be sin (or to become a sin offering) for us. Two truths are readily apparent from these verses. Number one, we are sinful; number two, we have been estranged from God.

Some people assume that everything is fine between

them and God and perceive no estrangement. As far as their sins are concerned, they care little, and furthermore, they don't really think God is very perturbed about them either. Such people have never bothered being reconciled or having their sins forgiven. Why not? Because they have never been awestruck by the immensity of their sins and the awfulness of their estrangement from God. Because, in short, they have an inaccurate understanding of who God is.

Moreover, Paul reminds us of our accountability to God for the lives that we have lived. There is no such thing as sloughing off our responsibilities. There is no such thing as avoiding accountability. In our "enlightened" age, people are very skilled at shuffling responsibility. We say, "I'm the person I am because of my parents. I'm the person I am because of my poor environment. I'm the person I am because of the traumatic events of my childhood." And no question about it, these are determining factors. But having said that, we must never forget that we and we alone are accountable for our decisions.

For instance, the Bible speaks quite clearly and forcibly about homosexuality, and calls it sin. Yet some people today would counter, "Homosexuals are victims of circumstances." Others might argue, "Homosexuals are not victims, just people with different sexual preferences to which they are completely entitled. And besides, when you look into their backgrounds, you will see why that preference is attractive to them." Background, environment, parental emphasis, all these things may well be contributory factors to homosexual tendencies. Equally, there is no doubt that Scripture says our tendencies come from a variety of sources, *but* the decision to engage in any activity known to be against the law of God is sin. We must bring ourselves under the scrutiny of God's revelation of Himself and evaluate ourselves in that light. Only then will we begin to accurately understand God and ourselves. Only then will we truly understand society's lostness, humanity's inability to rectify its spiritual ills.

Recently, I reread some of Jonathan Edwards' works. Among his writings is the very famous sermon entitled, "Sinners in the Hands of an Angry God." It is a classic piece of literature in America now and I was surprised when my children were required to read it in high school. I asked Dave, our eldest son, "How did the teacher handle it?"

"As a joke," he replied.

"How did the kids handle it?"

"Oh, they thought he was kind of weird and quaint, what with all the funny language."

How sad. They had totally missed the point. Jonathan Edwards was speaking about the awfulness of the human condition, the awesomeness of God, and the absolute necessity for people to recognize their lostness before God and their inability to put things right. And he graphically portrayed that fact when he said that man is no more capable of standing before the judgment of God than a spider's web is capable of capturing a rock as it falls off a mountain. We, in all our best intentions, we, in all our highest endeavors, we, in all our noblest desires, are totally incapable of bearing up under the awesome holiness, righteousness, justice, and judgment of God. We just can't do it, any more than a spider's web can capture a rock. We need to be confronted afresh with this message so that we might have an accurate understanding of God, of ourselves, and of our society.

Of course, it's one thing to have an accurate understanding. It's an entirely different thing to respond appropriately—with the fear of the Lord.

I had the privilege of being brought up in a situation that every small boy on the face of the earth would envy. We've all heard the expression, "as happy as a kid in a candy store." I was brought up in a candy store. Well, actually in the home just behind it. Every time I went out of our house, I walked past the candy counter. Every time I came back in, I walked past the candy counter. But I had been taught from my earliest days that the candy was not mine. If my parents gave permission, I could have a piece; otherwise, I wasn't even to touch it.

One day when nobody was around, I walked past the counter and the temptation was just too much to bear. I popped some candy into my mouth. What I didn't know, however, was that my father was behind a display of produce, and that he had made a peephole to enable him to keep an eye on the store while working behind the counter cutting cheese and butter. Suddenly I heard a voice saying, "Stuart, come here." If it had been the voice of God Himself, I would not have been more dumbstruck. I was totally flummoxed. I didn't know which way to go.

Now, my father wore a white apron which, for reasons known only to my mother, was starched daily. It was blindingly bright, tied in the front, with a big bow from which dangled long apron strings. And to give some idea how big I was at the time, I had just recently announced that I was as high as Daddy's "shop rope," which meant I had reached the level of his navel.

As I walked, very subdued, before him, I remember vividly the awful starched whiteness before my eyes. The depth of his voice seemed to come from the height of heaven, and the effect was awe-inspiring. Then he gave me a talk about whose sweets they were, about what I was to do if I wanted one, about the fact that I had taken one without permission. He went on to remind me that my action was stealing; that thieves are grown men who start out as little boys who steal candies; and that if I continued, I would end up in prison. (And I recall thinking to myself, "We've come a long way from one candy to prison.") Nevertheless, he got the message across. It was stern. It was straight. It came from high up—that impeccable knot right in front of my eyes! The impact was phenomenal, and I can promise you, I never took another candy again. That episode taught me, more powerfully than any other, that you don't touch what isn't yours.

The reason I was able to handle that kind of fatherly

reprimand was the look of love in his eyes. His sternness and straightness, his justice and judgment were not divorced from his love. I knew he was right, and as a small boy, I responded to it. Each of us must come to see God like that—in the reality of His person. And then we must respond to Him in an appropriate way.

The Prophet Isaiah is a prime example of how a man responds appropriately to a vision of God. He writes, "I saw the Lord sitting on a throne, high and lifted up, and the train of His robe filled the temple. . . . And one [angel] cried to another and said: 'Holy, holy, holy is the Lord of hosts; the whole earth is full of His glory!' " (Isaiah 6:1, 3, NKJV) What happened next? Isaiah fell on his face before the Lord and said, "I am ruined! For I am a man of unclean lips, and I live among a people of unclean lips" (verse 5). The prophet's right understanding of God resulted in reverence to the Lord—as seen in his sense of smallness in the presence of divine immensity; as seen in his silence before divine authority; as seen in his sense of shame in the presence of divine purity. That's what it means to reverence the Lord.

Sometimes we have the feeling, or we project the idea, that we are the center of the universe, that we are the ones who really matter, that everything revolves around us. Our interests, our conversations, our attitudes, our actions clearly demonstrate that this is the case. There is no thought of smallness. We are the bee's knees, the cat's meow, number one, *numero uno.*

But when we have a right understanding of God, smallness in the presence of His immensity is appropriate. Nothing more and nothing less. Our conversations are generously sprinkled with the words *me*, *my*, and *mine*. But when we rightly understand the Lord, in all His righteousness and justice, a strange silence falls upon our lips. Suddenly we recognize how puny are our concerns and how inaccurate are our judgments.

And then there develops a sense of shame for our sinfulness in the presence of divine purity. When we really begin to understand the whiteness of white, the purity of pureness, and the holiness of the holy God; when we begin to get a feel for who He is; when an image of His magnificence dawns on us, then our response will truly be God-honoring.

Jonathan Edwards sparked the Great Awakening in New England when he preached sermons like "Sinners in the Hands of an Angry God"—sermons that we now laugh at and ridicule in our high schools. Interestingly, that wasn't the reaction of the high school kids and the other people who heard the message firsthand. People began to cry out. They confessed aloud their sins. Some were so overcome that they fainted in the aisles. Was it all the result of rank emotionalism? No, Jonathan Edwards held his sermon notes in front of his face and read them in a loud, monotonous voice. And they were long! Most contemporary sermons would only be the introduction to one of his. He used very few illustrations and lots of solid theology. But as he preached about the awesomeness and holiness, the purity and righteousness of God, people were converted to faith in Jesus Christ. And as they left the church, they were heard going to their homes crying out, begging divine forgiveness, asking God to turn their lives around.

It happened once. It can happen again. Once people have a true understanding of God—repentance, reverence, and renewal are the supernatural responses.

Let's look for a moment at what hinders this proper understanding of God. David writes of the unbeliever, "There is no fear of God before his eyes. For in his own eyes he flatters himself too much to detect or hate his sin" (Psalm 36:1-2). What a remarkable statement that is. When an individual has no fear of the Lord, it is because the Lord is puny in his or her thinking. When I am absolutely absorbed with myself and the Lord is peripheral, if relevant at all, then it is highly probable I'll be so self-enamored I will neither detect nor hate my own sin. Obviously, I can't hate it if I can't detect it. But there is the possibility that I might detect it and simply excuse it.

Not so with a response of reverence. For through the work of the Spirit, revealing to me who God is, I detect the reality of sin in my life. Having detected it for what it is, I then am prepared to reject it for what it is. I am prepared to throw out the pat excuses: "I am the unfortunate victim of circumstances," "it is unavoidable," "it's just too bad," "it's a sickness." I'll call it what the Bible calls it—sin. Why? Because I will have a tremendously overwhelming sense of the holiness, righteousness, and justice of God. And when I do, I'll gladly deny self.

Preparing to write this chapter, I read all kinds of books and magazines, both theological and secular, and on five different occasions came across articles written by Daniel Yankelovich, a professor of psychology at New York University. After completing extensive research on American society, Yankelovich reports a dramatic switch in philosophical emphasis in the last two decades. Self-denial, he said, used to be a fundamental of American society, but no longer. Self-endorsement is the current line. He summarizes his findings by saying, "By concentrating day and night on your feelings, potentials, needs, wants, and desires, and by learning to assert them more freely, you do not become a freer, more spontaneous, more creative self. You become a narrower, more self-centered, more isolated one. You do not grow; you shrink" (*New Rules: Searching for Self-Fulfillment in a World Turned Upside Down*, Random House, p. 242). That's a psychologist, not a theologian, talking!

An underlying problem in a society that refuses self-denial is simply this: an inadequate understanding of self-ishness and sin. And underlying that is an inadequate grasp of who God is. When there is fear of the Lord, man knows himself. He is prepared to deny himself. He is prepared to detect his sin, reject it, and call upon God for His mercy and grace, full of reverence and repentance.

An accurate understanding of God will also fuel spiritual renewal, evidenced in part by a renewed desire to learn. I love what David writes in Psalm 34:11, "Come, my children, listen to me, I will teach you the fear of the Lord."

Our generation is producing superb ballet dancers and computer whizzes, wonder kids who excel at sports and are snappy dressers. And there's nothing wrong with that. But the horror is that we're producing an increasingly erudite, skilled, sophisticated society that is far removed from a sense of who God is or what man is before Him. They lack an appropriate response to the fear of the Lord.

When people truly grasp the fear of the Lord, they are so concerned about it, they teach it to their children. And from their earliest days, the children know who the Lord really is. They learn what it means to respond to Him in reverence, in repentance, and to have a constantly renewed desire to honor Him. That's how to recognize people who fear the Lord—they love to learn more of the fear of the Lord.

The fear of the Lord is not only something we learn but something we choose. According to Proverbs 1:29, some people "hated knowledge and did not choose to fear the Lord."

It still happens today. For instance, some men and women are, as they put it in modern parlance, "running around" or "fooling around." In other words, they're adulterers. These people freely engage in adulterous relationships, yet they take great pains to make sure their spouses and bosses don't find out. Why? Because it might affect how things go at home; it may affect their promotion. They're quite happy going ahead with the double standard as long as they can hide it from the only people who matter. Of course, it never occurs to them that God knows and that He sees. It never occurs to them that they're accountable. It never occurs to them that God calls adultery sin, and that, therefore, He is the One to whom they are ultimately responsible. They choose to block God out. They choose to discount what God says. They choose *not* to fear the Lord.

On the other hand, the person who fears the Lord is willing to learn more about that motivating factor, is willing to choose rightly, and is prepared to recognize that the fear of the Lord will teach him to "avoid evil" (Proverbs 16:6).

Not infrequently, people come to me in great distress because their families are falling apart. The reason their families are falling apart is that one or more family members is engaged in inappropriate behavior that started in a small way. Take, for example, a couple who begins to mistreat each other in their marriage. After a while, they tend to take the situation for granted. Instead of facing their problems, they simply ignore them. Then those problems multiply and get out of hand until, in the end, the husband and wife just give up and walk away. If only they had recognized from the start that the Lord is the One to whom they were accountable for their marriage, they would have taken much more care with the "little things."

Why do people get burned? They get too close to the fire. Why do they get too close to the fire? They like flirting with fire. They like the warmth of the fire and they figure they can enjoy its warmth yet avoid its danger. They refuse to believe that if they keep on getting closer and closer to the fire, they'll get burned, and eventually be destroyed. Praise God, however, that the fear of the Lord helps us to avoid this. The fear of the Lord is indeed the beginning of wisdom.

Is one of the motivating factors in *your* life a tremendous sense of reverence for the Lord? Are what you do and what you don't do governed by a tremendous sense of need for repentance and renewal by the Holy Spirit? Is your lifestyle directly attributable to the fact that you will stand before the Lord one day and give an account of the life you have lived? This is so important. Whatever other motivational factors might be operative in your life, make absolutely certain that the fear of the Lord is not missing.

HOW DOES THE FEAR OF THE LORD MOTIVATE?

What happens when the fear of the Lord is at work within a Christian? First of all, it produces *disciplined living*.

According to Exodus 20 and Deuteronomy 6, the Ten Commandments were given by God to His covenant people to help them learn the fear of the Lord and to keep them from sinning. And those who reverenced the Lord did just that. Yet stop people in any congregation on any Sunday morning and ask them to quote the Ten Commandments, and some won't be able to do it. The Ten Commandments have fallen by the wayside. But the people who fear the Lord recognize His commandments and are motivated to discipline their lives accordingly.

Secondly, fear of the Lord produces not only disciplined living but *holy living*. Paul exhorts the Corinthians, "Let us purify ourselves from everything that contaminates body and spirit, perfecting holiness out of reverence for God" (2 Corinthians 7:1). (*Reverence* here is the same word for *fear.*) People who fear the Lord aspire to holiness. They want to live holy lives.

The next time you go for a job interview and the interviewers sit there seriously and solemnly and ask you your ambitions, tell them, "I would love to live a holy life." Watch three Adam's apples disappear straight down three throats. High school kids, when you have to write that marvelous "My Ambition in Life" paper for your English class, express that your goal is to be holy. I guarantee your teacher will take the paper to the staff room where the faculty will have a wonderful giggle about it—at least many of them. Why? Because people don't think along those lines. Because striving to be holy doesn't enter our thinking. We are not born with a desire to be holy. We don't grow up with a desire to be holy. Holiness is something foreign to us.

How then will it come? When we understand the holiness of God, when we understand that we came from the holy God, go to the holy God, and survive because of the holy God, then the desire to be holy begins. We want to please Him and our aspirations turn to holiness. New yearnings are born in our lives. The Holy Spirit carefully prepares us to purify ourselves from everything that contaminates body and spirit. What a difference this new attitude makes.

Our society is characterized by lax living, flippancy, and superficiality. And these attitudes have become rampant in the fellowship of believers. But when we are willing to acknowledge that God is neither impressed nor pleased with us, when we accept the fact that we will stand before Him and give an account for the lives that we have lived, then we begin to manifest reverence. And our reverence engenders repentance, which, in turn, engenders a desire for renewal. The fear of the Lord leads inevitably to disciplined and holy living.

Thirdly, fear of the Lord produces *concerned living*. Let's return for a moment to our text, 2 Corinthians 5: "Since, then, we know what it is to fear the Lord, we try to persuade men. . . . We are therefore Christ's ambassadors, as though God were making His appeal through us. We implore you on Christ's behalf: be reconciled to God" (verses 11, 20). What's happening here? Paul says, because we understand the fear of the Lord, we are concerned about people and we seek ways to demonstrate that concern.

There is a monumental lack of concern in the church of Jesus Christ today for people who don't know Christ. It is relatively easy to institute programs in the church that are going to make comfortable Christians more comfortable. It's an entirely different thing, however, to get Christians motivated or mobilized to reach out to people who don't know the Lord. And one reason is that we don't really honestly believe that they're lost. We don't really believe in the judgment of God, and therefore, we don't really believe that they need to be reconciled to God, repent of their sin, and accept Christ.

The fear of the Lord shows itself in a commitment to missions. It shows itself in a commitment to evangelism. It shows itself in wise use of time. If we honestly, genuinely believed in the lostness of humanity, the sinfulness of their estate, and the inevitability of judgment for them, we would demonstrably reapportion our time to reach these men, women, and children with the Gospel. Certainly we've got to be balanced at this point, but often the imbalance comes because of a lack of fear of the Lord and a lack of fear for those who don't fear the Lord.

Finally, the fear of the Lord produces a real sense of *corporate living*. I love what Paul says in Ephesians 5, that marvelous passage that husbands love to quote to their wives: "Wives, submit to your husbands." I can just imagine all the men reading this and smiling and all the women looking glum. Hang on, ladies, hang on! Before Paul ever talks about wives submitting to their husbands, what does he talk about? He talks about us submitting ourselves to one another *in the fear of the Lord* (Ephesians 5:21). So frankly, I don't want to hear another word from the men telling their wives to submit to them until I can see those same men submitted to the Lord in deep reverence.

And notice something else in this Ephesians passage; we submit to one another out of reverence for the Lord. Why? Because every person we deal with is someone God made. We can't just move people around like we're shuffling bodies. We are dealing with beings of infinite and eternal consequence, created by God, and we'll answer to Him for the way we handle them.

I know for a fact that we could cut the divorce rate dramatically if people would simply fear the Lord in their marriages, if they honestly believed in their hearts they're going to answer to Him for what they're doing. And I'm also firmly convinced that we could dramatically improve all our marriages if we would bring a sense of reverence for the Lord to our relationships with each other. We would treat each other properly because we would know that the Lord holds us accountable.

Not only would marriages be improved, but we would see dramatic changes in the church as well. Saul of Tarsus created absolute havoc in the Christian church. His dauntless persecution of believers was dreadful. Then God solved the problem—Saul was converted. According to Acts 9:31,

Luke says that *then* the church had peace. Not that they put their feet up, their hands behind their heads, and sighed, "Oh, what a break!" No, the church used the sudden freedom to move ahead. They simply substituted the fear of Saul of Tarsus for the fear of the Lord. It was a very sensible thing to do, because Jesus once said words to this effect: "Listen, folks. Don't fear man, who can kill the body. Rather fear God who, after the body has been killed, can cast the soul into hell." That's perspective, and that's Jesus speaking.

What a lovely thing it is for the church of Jesus Christ to live in the fear of the Lord. When people respond to each other, not on the basis of like or dislike or agreement or disagreement, but on the basis of accountability to the Lord, then we see real concern. What an exciting thing to find a church that walks in the fear of the Lord. What an exciting thing to find a marriage lived in the fear of the Lord. What a delightful thing it is to rightly understand the Lord and appropriately respond to Him. It's a powerful motivating factor.

The key to it all is a balanced view of God. God is much more than a delightful, warm fuzzy. Of course He is warm; of course He is gracious; of course He is merciful; of course He is loving; of course He is creative. But He is also holy, just, and righteous—our judge. Therefore, if we're to live rightly before Him, both "sides" must be built into our understanding. Only then will we incorporate a proper fear of the Lord in our relationship with Him.

Though we're very much aware of our own inability to grasp God's holiness, majesty, and immensity, we can trust the Holy Spirit to convey to our open, receptive hearts that which we need to know. And as we place our trust in Him, He will lead us to a right understanding of both God and ourselves.

When this happens, then we can rightly reverence God, live repentantly before Him, and recognize in the renewal of our hearts that He really is producing disciplined, holy, concerned lives which demonstrate, among other things that we are motivated by the fear of the Lord.

PERSONAL REFLECTION
It would be incorrect for me to suggest that I am always motivated by love and gratitude and a sense of privilege. Frankly, I am not and I'm glad to be reminded that You, Lord, are awesome, deserving respect and humble obedience. Help me to learn more of what it means to fear the Lord, because that is the true beginning of wisdom.

"Therefore, since through God's mercy we have this ministry, we do not lose heart. Rather, we have renounced secret and shameful ways; we do not use deception, nor do we distort the Word of God. On the contrary, by setting forth the truth plainly we commend ourselves to every man's conscience in the sight of God. And even if our Gospel is veiled, it is veiled to those who are perishing. The god of this age has blinded minds of the unbelievers, so that they cannot see the light of the Gospel of the glory of Christ, who is the image of God. For we do not preach ourselves, but Jesus Christ as Lord, and ourselves as your servants for Jesus' sake. For God, who said, 'Let light shine out of darkness,' made His light shine in our hearts to give us the light of the knowledge of the glory of God in the face of Christ.

"But we have this treasure in jars of clay to show that this all-surpassing power is from God and not from us. We are hard pressed on every side, but not crushed; perplexed, but not in despair; persecuted, but not abandoned; struck down, but not destroyed. We always carry around in our body the death of Jesus, so that the life of Jesus may also be revealed in our body. For we who are alive are always being given over to death for Jesus' sake, so that His life may be revealed in our mortal body. So then, death is at work in us, but life is at work in you."

2 CORINTHIANS 4:1-12

eight
KEEPING ON
KEEPING ON

I'm not quite sure how long the term *burnout* has been around, but it seemed to impact my corner of the world for the first time a couple of years ago. Now whenever I hear the word, I am very much aware of what is happening in many people's lives. They're tired to the point of exhaustion. They're discouraged to the point of quitting. And, in many instances, I am sure there are good reasons why they feel this way.

However, as is usually the case, the term *burnout* began to work its way out of the exclusive realm of the secular world and into Christianity. And when it began to appear in the Christian vocabulary, I began to get alarmed, for this whole concept of Christian burnout is something that needs to be very carefully addressed.

I'm old enough to remember when we used to sing the hymn, "Let Me Burn Out for Thee, Dear Lord." But there's a marked difference, I think, between burning out *in* Christian experience and deciding with honesty and sincerity that we would much prefer to burn out *for* the Lord Jesus. Where is the balance? What should the real situation be?

No question about it, the Bible has much to say about the need to maintain our spiritual experience, about the need to continually and consistently progress in our Christian walk. The Bible also has much to say about our need to keep on keeping on. This in itself is a very powerful Christian motivation. When non-Christians respond to their trying circumstances by quitting, Christians are called to persevere, to endure. Something inside, something supernatural allows them to transcend their circumstances and achieve things that, in many other situations, they would never achieve. It is quite clear that this is what's expected of believers.

The Apostle Paul's life and teachings wonderfully illustrate this principle of keeping on. So once again we turn to this model of motivation to see what made him tick, in order that we might be encouraged and instructed ourselves.

PAUL'S REALITY

First of all, let's examine the reality of Paul's lifestyle. In his second letter to the Corinthians, he picks up momentum and develops a certain rhythm in chapter 4, verses 8-10. He writes, "We are hard pressed on every side, but not crushed; perplexed, but not in despair; persecuted, but not abandoned; struck down, but not destroyed."

Notice immediately the Apostle Paul is not suggesting that his spiritual experience is a bed of roses. It is unfortunate that sometimes preachers, in their enthusiasm, have encouraged people to become Christians by assuring them that if they do, everything will be hunky-dory. If we give people the impression that Christianity will exempt them from all the problems and difficulties of life, we are grossly misleading them. We must stand firmly against this kind of deception.

Some time ago, the expression *the victorious Christian life* was in vogue. Unfortunately, this phrase implied that a true Christian lived in a state of constant victory. Everything was always marvelous—a smile on your face and a song in your heart. However, thinking people soon realized that the only way to truly experience *a victory* is by first having *a battle*.

So, let's get it straight. God never called us to a rose garden. God never suggested to us that the Christian life would be anything less than a struggle. In fact, repeatedly in Scripture we are told that it is going to be a rough, tough situation. But, in the roughness and the toughness of it all, in the challenge of the fight, we are to keep on keeping on.

Back to Paul. He says he is hard pressed on every side, but not crushed. What this means literally is that he's a bit like a quarterback who suddenly finds his offensive line collapsing around him while the other team is blitzing everybody. He's absolutely surrounded by his opponents, but they aren't able to tackle him. Such is Paul's situation.

Two illustrations here will suffice. Shortly after Paul was converted, he entered the city of Damascus. Some people there plotted to take his life, but the believers gathered protectively around him. As the opposing forces cornered him in his hideaway, Paul jumped into a basket. Then his friends tied a rope to it and lowered him out of the window, down the city wall, allowing him to escape into the night. What a lovely example of what it meant for Paul to be pressed on every side but not crushed. In football terminology, he escaped from the pocket and the blitz failed one more time.

On Paul's last visit to Jerusalem he also was hemmed in on every side. First he was rescued from a rioting crowd. But before he could relax, another plot on his life was in the works. However, word got out; the authorities were informed; the cavalry and the infantry were literally called out; and at 9 at night the army encircled Paul and marched him all the way to Caesarea and safety. Once again, pressed on every side, but not crushed. Paul's Christian life was certainly not easy. Yet he was always able to keep going.

Next Paul says that he is "perplexed, but not in despair." The idea here is one of stretching. Paul encountered situation after situation where he felt he was being stretched totally out of shape, not knowing which way to go. But like the rubber band that is stretched yet doesn't snap, so Paul was stretched and stretched but always able to testify to the fact that never, ever was he in a position of having given up.

In 2 Corinthians 1, Paul reminds his readers of the tremendous problems he had in Asia, problems so great he despaired even of life. Paul was totally beyond anything that he could handle by himself, feeling that there was absolutely no way he could survive the difficulty. But survive it he did. Notice the picture again. Pressed but not crushed; stretched but not snapped.

What more could Paul endure? Well, he was "persecuted, but not abandoned." The word translated *persecuted* here is also translated *hunted* or *pursued,* and there is an obvious link. If you like to go hunting, you soon realize that what you're hunting doesn't feel particularly happy about it. In fact, the object of your hunt has every right to feel persecuted. And that is just the idea in the New Testament Greek rendering. Paul says he felt that he was hounded all the time, and even so, he was never abandoned. He never felt, at any given moment, that the Lord had left him—and that was a tremendous inner resource.

Paul's vision of the Macedonian inviting him to come over to Macedonia was not entirely a "red carpet" affair. Upon arriving in Philippi, the apostle was almost immediately imprisoned, then beaten, and finally kicked out of the city. Subsequently, he made his way to Thessalonica, where he was very encouraged by the response of the people. Unfortunately, the rabble-rousers from Philippi followed him to Thessalonica and chased him out of town there too! Undaunted, Paul went to Berea. Once there, he found people who were, he said, very noble and gracious. They assiduously studied what he had to say to see if he spoke the truth. Paul was again greatly encouraged. But then, those malcontents from Philippi hounded him out of Berea. He escaped to Athens. When he got into Athens, the folks there made it abundantly clear that they were not prepared to accept him. So Paul left Athens and went to Corinth where he got into all kinds of problems. But there the Lord appeared to him and said, "Don't worry, Paul. I have many people in this place." It's not hard to see why this idea of being hounded all the time was very real to Paul. Yet after all this, he is able to say, "I was never abandoned."

Next Paul confesses that he was "struck down, but not destroyed." Using a boxing analogy here, we might say that Paul was frequently down on the canvas, but his enemies never were able to knock him out. He was always able to get back on his feet.

Remember Paul's visits to Iconium, Lystra, and Derbe. On one occasion the people were so incensed by his preaching that they started to stone him. And so severe was the beating that they dragged him outside the city gate assuming he was dead. But then Paul miraculously recovered. He was down, but not out. He picked himself up, headed straight back into town, and concluded the message that had been so rudely interrupted.

This type of determination and character may be foreign to us, but this is the lifestyle Paul lived. And though we may have a little difficulty identifying with it, we have no difficulty at all understanding what he's saying. Despite adversity, he is determined to keep on keeping on for Jesus' sake. There's great resilience in Paul's words, great power, phenomenal perseverance and endurance.

Paul goes into more detail about his hardships later in the same epistle: "As servants of God, we commend ourselves in every way: in great endurance; in troubles, hardships, and distresses [triplet 1]; in beatings, imprisonments, and riots [triplet 2]; in hard work, sleepless nights, and hunger [triplet 3]" (2 Corinthians 6:4-5).

Let's look at these three triplets a bit more specifically. The first refers to the many troubles that Paul was subjected to. Physical problems. Mental problems. Spiritual problems. In 2 Corinthians 11:23-28 he speaks very openly about these things. You think you have problems! Listen to Paul's. He was flogged severely, imprisoned frequently, and exposed to death time and time again. Five times he received thirty-nine lashes from the Jews. Three times he was beaten by the Romans with rods. He was stoned. Three times he was shipwrecked. He spent a day and a night on the open sea. He was constantly on the move; in danger from rivers, bandits, his own countrymen, Gentiles, and false prophets. He was in danger in the city, in the country, and at sea. He labored long hours and often went without sleep. He knew hunger and thirst, cold and nakedness. And on top of all that, he was daily concerned for the various churches he planted. This guy knows what pressure is. He's talking about life.

Paul's physical problems, his mental and emotional strife, his spiritual anguish are enough to make anybody say, "I've had it! I'm through!" But Paul says, "For Christ's sake, I delight in weaknesses, in insults, in hardships, in persecutions, in difficulties. For when I am weak, then I am strong" (2 Corinthians 12:10).

Secondly, Paul mentions hardships. In our society we have been led to believe that every problem has a solution. We've also been led to expect that every solution is relatively easy, instantaneous, and cheap. But every problem does not have a solution. Even if solutions do exist, many of them don't come easily, few come cheaply, and rarely are they instantaneous. Christians ought to know this, but one of the frightening trends in contemporary Christianity is that we seem to be overlooking this whole issue. We want so hard to deny hardships, the kinds of things Paul says are normal.

Paul carries this theme one step further by talking about distresses. The word he uses here for *distresses* means literally "getting locked into situations." That happened to him repeatedly—and literally—in prison, but it also happened when he got himself into trouble with the authorities. And Paul was always clashing with the authorities. He got himself into trouble with the ecclesiastical authorities. He got himself into trouble with people who were stubborn and inflexible. He continually became locked into problems with seemingly no resolutions. And what did he do? He kept on keeping on.

The second triplet (2 Corinthians 6:5) deals more in depth with the physical pressures Paul experienced from his opponents. The beatings, the imprisonments, and the riots all resulted from Paul's stand for the Gospel. And then the final triplet (verse 5) deals with the sheer mental and emotional pressure of the work. Don't get any glamorous ideas about the life of an apostle. Paul says being an apostle means hard work and sleepless nights. And when you *do* get to bed, frequently you haven't had time to eat. Yet he talks about these situations unabashedly and without boasting because his brothers and sisters in Christ need to know the facts. It is this man who is encouraging all of us to recognize the necessity of pressing on in our own difficult circumstances—to keep on keeping on.

"Well, that was the Apostle Paul," we might say, "and you expect that toughness from those kinds of guys." Or we might contend, "Well, of course, his circumstances are totally unrelated to mine. But let him experience my 20th-century problems and see how he handles them!" But the point is not to compare his circumstances with ours. The point is simply to understand that Paul is saying the Christian life is a struggle to the end—full of pressures. Nevertheless, we believers must behave differently from unbelievers who find themselves in similar situations.

PAUL'S REACTION
With that in mind, let's next look at how the Apostle Paul reacts to his reality. First of all, on two occasions he says, "We do not lose heart" (2 Corinthians 4:1, 16). Paul surely

had many grounds for being discouraged, many reasons for quitting. But he just didn't do it.

Have you ever been in a situation where you felt you just couldn't go on? I once heard Christian writer and speaker Olan Hendrix tell the story about taking his wife to Africa. And he said, with his wife sitting in the front row, "My wife thinks that 'slumming it' is staying in a Holiday Inn." To no one's surprise, Mrs. Hendrix hated Africa. She couldn't wait to go home. But there was one thing Olan knew would excite her. He had been to Victoria Falls and had stood at the end of the falls and seen the magnificent bronze statue of David Livingstone, the first white man ever to view that awesome sight. So he kept his wife going through the entire trip by reminding her of Victoria Falls.

At last they reached this long-anticipated stop on the journey, and Olan Hendrix pointed with pride to the statue of Livingstone, the great missionary-statesman-explorer who stands shading his eyes, peering out over the falls. This was the moment Olan had been waiting for. Turning to his wife he said, "There you are. There is David Livingstone. Look at him peering out over the falls. What do you think he is thinking?"

Mrs. Hendrix replied, "I think he's thinking, 'I've had it up to here with Africa.'"

The story may be funny, but the expression isn't. "I've had it up to here with my kids." "I've had it up to here with my marriage." "I've had it up to here with my job." "I've had it up to here with..."

Could we please have a moratorium on "I've-had-it-up-to-here's?" And could we instead start showing some Christ-like stick-to-itiveness which simply says, "Hey, listen, I sometimes feel as if I'm pressed, but I'm not going to be crushed; I'm stretched, but I'm not going to be snapped; I'm hounded, but I'll never be abandoned; I may be down, but they're not going to count me out; and I know the pressure of circumstances, opponents, and work, but I'm not going to lose heart." That's real Christian motivation. And that's how we can be different in our world today.

Another clue to the Apostle Paul's reaction to his reality is found in 2 Corinthians 6:4, where he writes, "As servants of God we commend ourselves in every way: *in great endurance*" (italics added). In other words, his reaction to adversity is not only the refusal to lose heart but the commitment to endure as a believer in all that life brings his way.

Some time ago, I ran in a ten-kilometer race. The contestants were an interesting lot. Some were dressed up as beer bottles or bananas. Others carried beds and all kinds of weird stuff. And then there were the people who were obviously very serious runners. As we started out, I could hardly move or hear myself think, I was so hedged in by people. Everyone was laughing and joking and waving to friends. Some were running backward, and some were skipping, intent on having fun. The noise of thousands of voices was amazing.

That was the scene for the first quarter of a mile. Then the noise abated somewhat. After about half a mile, the prominent sound was the rhythmic flap-flap of feet. At the mile marker, I couldn't hear feet flapping, just lots of panting. And after a mile and a half, it became unusually quiet. I was running with Judy, my daughter, and all of a sudden it seemed we were the only ones there. I looked around and saw that the crowd had thinned out.

I discovered afresh that morning something about running—and about the Christian life. There were far more people at the start of that race than at the finish line. Lots and lots of people started—fooling around, goofing off, laughing, and giggling, but none of that counted. What counts is not how you start the race, but how you finish it. What counts in the spiritual realm is not how you start out, but how you finish up. The reality of your start is determined by the reality of your finish. That's what Jesus meant when He said, "He who endures to the end will be saved" (Matthew 10:22, NKJV).

Recall the Lord Jesus' Parable of the Sower in Matthew 13. Some of the seed landed on hard ground, some on stony ground, some among thorns, and some in fertile soil. And what were the results of this sowing? When the seed fell on hard ground, the heat came and shriveled it. When it fell on stony ground, the birds of the air came and plucked it away. When it fell on thorny ground, sharp thistles and weeds grew up and choked it. But when it fell on good ground, it sprouted forth and reproduced itself.

The people who listened to Jesus said, "What are you talking about?"

And the Lord explained in words to this effect: "Some people listen to what God says, but immediately thereafter, because of their minimal interest, the devil snatches the Word away like a big, old bird. And other people are so caught up with all kinds of concerns—their money, how they look, what's happening to their kids—that they're really not interested in spiritual things, so the Word of God gets choked before it can take root. And in other people the seeds of the Gospel spring up instantaneously, have a marvelous start, but when the heat's on, they just fizzle. The real producers are the people who, when the seed of the Word falls into their hearts, allow it to take root, bear fruit, and keep on bearing fruit."

What our Lord Jesus is saying is this: all kinds of people come under Christian influence. The thing that determines the validity of their Christian experience, however, is not that they're under Christian influence, nor that they made an initial profession, nor that they started out with a great flash; but that they are rooted and grounded in God's truth and endure through thick and thin. The reality of their experience is shown not in how they start, but in the way they finish.

The word *perseverance* isn't mentioned much nowadays because the concept is not very popular. Who wants to persevere? We'd rather trade it in. We'd rather act "mature," admit we made a mistake, and start again. Who wants to stick to something? We'd prefer to be happy with our immediate circumstances, but if we're not, then we can always change our circumstances.

In opposition to this, the Bible teaches that people who are truly the Lord's endure. They persevere. They keep on keeping on. When the heat comes and the birds come and the thorns come, the Lord's people hang in there because they are deeply grounded in Him. How and why does this happen? Theologians tell us that the reason we can persevere in the Lord is simply because the Lord is committed to persevering with us.

After Jesus tells the multitude at Capernaum that He is the Bread of Life, He tells them something equally powerful and compelling. He says, "All that the Father gives Me will come to Me, and whoever comes to Me I will never drive away" (John 6:37). In the original Greek that verse reads like a double negative: "I will *never, no never,* drive them away." The Lord Jesus is totally committed to maintaining His relationship with those who are truly committed to Him. Likewise, Jesus the Good Shepherd promises, "My sheep listen to My voice; I know them, and they follow Me. I give them eternal life, and they shall never perish; no one can snatch them out of My hand. My Father, who has given them to Me, is greater than all; no one can snatch them out of My Father's hand. I and the Father are One" (John 10:27-29).

When I was a young boy, I remember a preacher who stayed in our home. One day he said to me, "Son, I want to show you something." He took a penny out of his pocket, put it on his palm, then held his finger over the top of it. "Now you're the penny, Stuart, and this hand is your Saviour, the Lord Jesus. You may fall in the hand of the Lord, but you won't fall out of the hand of the Lord. I'll tell you why."

Then he put his other hand over the one holding the coin, wrapping the first hand in the second. "Now," he said, "can you see the penny?"

"No. I know where it is though."

"Where is it?"

"Inside the first hand and inside the second hand."

The preacher nodded his head and explained, "The first hand is Jesus and the second hand is the Father. When you are in the hand of the Lord Jesus, no one can pluck you out of His hand, and when you're in the hand of the Father, absolutely no one can pluck you out of His hand. Therefore you are secure in the Father *and* the Son—and they are One."

And then he added something I've never forgotten. "Of course, that doesn't mean to say you can't fall, but it does mean that every time you fall, you fall in the pierced hand of the Lord Jesus, and it hurts both Him and you. And this in itself should be an encouragement to you to be secure in the Lord, but also to have a desire to go on with Him."

This is the same lesson Paul is teaching: endure in the Lord because the Lord is committed to being faithful to us. Paul puts the idea in dramatic words at the end of Romans 8: "I am convinced that neither death nor life, neither angels nor demons, neither the present nor the future, nor any powers, neither height nor depth, nor anything else in all creation, will be able to separate us from the love of God that is in Christ Jesus our Lord" (verses 38-39). Think of all the things this passage encompasses. Death and life. Angels and demons. Present and future. Any power imaginable. Height or depth or anything else in creation.

I took my wife, Jill, to the Milwaukee airport recently for a flight to Michigan. It was foggy that morning and the planes were nosing around in the fog. I asked Jill, "Can you remember when you were terrified to go on an airplane?"

"Sure," she admitted. "I think about it every time I get on one now."

"How do you feel?"

"I remember how I used to be so frightened."

"You're not frightened anymore?" I asked.

"No."

"Why not?"

And she answered, "Stuart, you know why."

Indeed I do. Jill began to believe what God says in His Word. "Neither height nor depth . . . [can] separate us from the love of God that is in Christ." We can fly as high as human technology allows; we can go as deep as submarines can submerge; we can be haunted by our past and fretful about the future; but nothing, absolutely nothing, either natural or supernatural, can separate us from God if we are truly committed to Him. We *will* endure in Him. Why? Because He *will* endure with us. That powerful truth sustained Paul. It can sustain you too.

What happens then with people who start off well and fizzle out? What happens with people who make a great profession and then show no interest at all? God knows their hearts, and it's not our responsibility to judge. But one thing we do know, the reality of our spiritual experience is not determined by how we start, but how we finish.

PAUL'S REASONING

We may be saying to ourselves at this point, "OK, Paul, you ended up in all these messes and yet you didn't lose heart. But how were you able to do it?"

To discover Paul's answer, we need to look at 2 Corinthians 4. The chapter starts off with the word *therefore*, which should automatically make us ask ourselves, "What's it there for?" It is there for the simple reason of linking what has gone before with what is coming. "Therefore since through God's mercy we have this ministry [we've been talking about], we do not lose heart."

One of the things Paul bears in mind continually is the fact of God's mercy in his life. He says a bit later, "God has shined in my heart and given me the light of the knowledge of Himself in the face of Jesus Christ. How gracious of Him!" (2 Corinthians 4:6) Paul remembers the days when he was a persecutor, when he was opposed to Christ, when he blasphemed the name of the Lord Jesus. But now he marvels in the knowledge that God actually reached out to him in mercy and touched his life, drawing Paul to Himself.

Let's think Paul's thoughts as he must have thought them: "He not only shined into my life; He not only gave me understanding and truth that I didn't have; but He also committed this ministry of apostleship to me. He has given me the inestimable privilege and the unspeakable joy of being able to share what He's done in my life. Of all the people He could have called, of all the people He could have touched, of all the people He could have entrusted with this ministry, He called me. He entrusted *me.*" Paul is overwhelmed with the mercy of God.

Anyone who understands God's mercy and grace, and anyone who realizes the tremendous sense of privilege of being exposed to the truth of the Gospel is a person who keeps on keeping on because he or she never, ever escapes from the wonder and thrill of it all.

A word of warning here. If you find no sense of wonder, no sense of thrill, no sense of conscious enjoyment and excitement about the truth of the Lord Jesus, then question yourself very seriously as to whether you possess any spiritual life or reality at all. (This is too serious a matter for you to let simply slide by.) It is this awareness of Christ's mercy that helps Paul react properly to the pressures of his life and this is his first reason to persevere.

A second reason for keeping on is a concern for Christ's honor. Notice two verses and two phrases within them. Paul writes, "We do not preach ourselves, but Jesus Christ as Lord, and ourselves as your servants *for Jesus' sake*" (2 Corinthians 4:5, italics added); "We who are alive are always being given over to death *for Jesus' sake* so that His life may be revealed in our mortal body" (verse 11, italics added).

Do you remember when you were a child and your mother and father taught you to pray? You probably prayed about the cat and the dog and the canary and the rain stopping and all sorts of other things; then you finished up with the words, "for Jesus' sake." As a toddler you probably didn't think about it. But it's possible you've continued the habit into adult life and you still end your prayers, "for Jesus' sake, Amen." If so, it's probably a healthy idea to ask yourself, "What on earth am I saying? What do those words mean?"

What Paul is saying is this: "I am your servant, not for my sake, not for what I get out of it; not for your sake, not for what you get out if it; but for His sake." Now the lovely thing about being the servant of the Corinthians for Jesus' sake is this: when Paul has had it up to here with Corinth, that's irrelevant. And when the Corinthians aren't very nice to him, that's irrelevant. Paul isn't there for his own sake; He's not even there for their sakes. He's there for Jesus' sake. Paul's sole reason to work among the Corinthians is so that the Corinthians might likewise fall in love with Jesus and give Him honor and praise.

Paul goes on to say he's not only committed to endure for Jesus' sake, but he's prepared to suffer for it too. Why? Because as he suffers, people will notice. "Why do you keep on keeping on? You owe it to yourself to take a break, to relax and take it easy," they'll probably say.

Then Paul will have the opportunity to tell them, "But I'm not in this for me; I'm in this for Jesus' sake."

The apostle looks at his circumstances and reacts by saying, "I do not lose heart." He listens to the complaints and criticisms and replies, "I endure all things." And his detractors wonder why and he responds: "Because I understand God's mercy and I'm concerned for Christ's honor. I'm doing it for Him."

Another reason for Paul's perseverance is his concern for eternal realities. In 2 Corinthians 4:16 he puts it this way: "Though outwardly we are wasting away, yet inwardly we are being renewed day by day." Paul is being very realistic about life. "Outwardly," he says, "I'm not the man I used to be." I can certainly identify with this! When my children come home for a visit, they love to get out the old pictures of me and say, "You're not the man you used to be, Dad." And, of course, they're right!

I distinctly remember teaching my kids to run. I also remember the day my eldest son took me out for a run and ran me into the ground. And then he had the audacity to turn around and say, "Dad, I don't like you letting me win."

I have a phenomenal memory. I can think back to when I had hair on the top of my head as well as on my chin! Now I just let it grow wherever it will. I can remember when I could see my congregation without my glasses. I can remember when I just needed one lens; now I have bifocals. It's only a matter of time until it's trifocals and in the end it'll be a magnifying glass! Yes, the outward man is perishing.

Let's look again at Paul. He used to scale the mountains and be the first to the summit. Now they have to push the old boy up there, urging him along. When he was ship-wrecked in the past, he used to be able to swim out to the life raft. Now they have to drag him to it. But when they finally get him to the top of the mountain or safely onto the life raft, what do they discover? The old codger is full of life! The outward man is perishing, yet the inward man is being renewed daily, daily, daily. And if you were to ask Paul why this is so, he'd reply as he does in 2 Corinthians 4:17-18, "For our light and momentary troubles are achieving for us an eternal glory that far outweighs them all. So we fix our eyes not on what is seen, but on what is unseen. For what is seen is temporary, but what is unseen is eternal."

If we were to interview Paul, we might ask him, "Paul, what do you mean by momentary troubles and light afflictions? What are you talking about?"

"I'm talking about being pressed, stretched, and hounded. Pressures from work, pressures from people, pressures from opposition."

"What do you call them?"

"I call them light and momentary afflictions."

"You've got to be kidding, Paul."

"No, no, I'm not kidding. You see, it's all a matter of perspective. If I concentrate on my troubles they become overwhelming. But the difficulties are temporary. I mean, I'm here for a time, but I'll be there for eternity. The things that God is doing in my life now are making me ready for life with Him forever. Compared to eternity, these present encumbrances are very light, relatively insignificant."

"We're beginning to understand what makes you tick, Paul. You really are concerned about Jesus' name being honored. And you really do think in terms of eternity, don't you?"

"Right."

"And you are overwhelmed by a sense of God's mercy."

"That's true."

"Anything else?"

"Oh yes. I've also had a vision of human need."

In 2 Corinthians 4:3-4 we see this vision revealed: "If our Gospel is veiled, it is veiled to those who are perishing. The god of this age has blinded the minds of unbelievers, so that they cannot see the light of the Gospel of the glory of Christ."

Spiritual realities are at work in our world that involve the forces of evil. These forces blind people's minds to the truth, and it is necessary for God to shine into their hearts. "Now," Paul says, "I can't be quitting when there are people in the grip of evil. I can't give up when there are people around me whose eyes are blinded. God wants to shine into their hearts." And so his concern for human souls is yet another important motivational factor, compelling him to persevere.

The final reason behind Paul's commitment to endure is seen in his dedication to God's glory, as illustrated in 2 Corinthians 4:7. Here he says, "We have this treasure [of the knowledge of Christ] in jars of clay to show the all-surpassing power is from God and not from us."

I wonder if at this point Paul is thinking of the story of

Gideon. Once his army was whittled down to 300 men, God told Gideon to give each man a trumpet, a clay jar with a light inside it, and a sword. Thus equipped, they surrounded the camp of the Midianites in the dead of night. And then, at a given signal, they blew their trumpets in unison and frightened the Midianites out of their wits. Next they crashed their clay jars to the ground and flooded the night sky with light. The startled Midianites thought they were surrounded and panicked. Then Gideon's army finished them off with their swords.

Paul seems to be saying, "As long as the clay jar is intact, the light doesn't shine out. But once the jar cracks and breaks, then the light shines through." And he makes a comparison with himself. "I'm an old clay pot, that's all. I'm not interested in patching up the cracks or painting the exterior. What I *am* interested in is seeing the old clay pot crack and break, if necessary, so that the excellency of the glory of God at work in my humble life may be seen. If something about the way I handle my affliction will glorify God, I welcome afflictions. If something about the way I respond to pressures demonstrates the power of God, then let the pressures continue."

Brave words indeed! Words from the lips of an extraordinary man. But his extraordinary abilities should not be allowed to obscure the ordinariness of his humanity. His physical pain hurt as much as anyone else's. His mental anguish was just as intense. But his reactions were above normal, because as an ordinary man he knew an extraordinary Christ—and that made all the difference.

Come to think of it, we know Him too. And that motivates us to keep on keeping on.

PERSONAL REFLECTION

I'm no Paul, Lord. But I am a redeemed individual committed to You—and that means You are committed to me. In light of this, I am very anxious to develop mature attitudes which will be demonstrated in courageous continuance upon the paths You lead me. Aid me in this desire for the sake of the Lord Jesus.

"For Christ's love compels us, because we are convinced that One died for all, and therefore all died. And He died for all, that those who live should no longer live for themselves but for Him who died for them and was raised again.

"So from now on we regard no one from a worldly point of view. Though we once regarded Christ in this way, we do so no longer. Therefore, if anyone is in Christ, he is a new creation; the old has gone, the new has come! All this is from God, who reconciled us to Himself through Christ and gave us the ministry of reconciliation: that God was reconciling the world to Himself in Christ, not counting men's sins against them. And He has committed to us the message of reconciliation. We are therefore Christ's ambassadors, as though God was making His appeal through us. We implore you on Christ's behalf: be reconciled to God."

2 CORINTHIANS 5:14-20

nine
FOR THE LOVE OF CHRIST

Christian motivation is unique because it vitally centers upon the relationship we have with Christ. If there is no relationship with Christ, we may be motivated by all manner of things, but we should never confuse such influences with Christian motivation. If, however, we are related to Christ, then we can expect to be motivated by factors quite different than the non-Christian. Nothing is clearer in this regard than the subject of this final chapter. It is what the Apostle Paul calls the love of Christ.

RECOGNIZING THE LOVE OF CHRIST

Nothing is more precious in our relationship with Christ than the recognition of His love. In fact, once understood, this love should so grip us that we become highly motivated by it. Other influences in our lives automatically will fall into second place. This is exactly what the Apostle Paul is driving at when he writes, "For the love of Christ [or, Christ's love] compels us" (2 Corinthians 5:14).

Let's explore the expression *the love of Christ* for a moment. Interestingly, the original Greek in this passage can be translated in one of two ways: to mean either

Christ's love for man or man's love for Christ. Now, the question before us is, which one is correct in this instance? The answer, of course, comes from looking at the context. And when we do, it's apparent that Paul is thinking about the love of Christ for mankind, for he goes on to talk about Christ becoming sin and dying for all.

Now, in all fairness, I must admit that Christ's love for man and man's love for Christ cannot be completely dissected, for the two are bound up in each other. In a sense, they are two sides of the same coin, for when we rightly understand the love of Christ for us, then the proper response is returning that love. Christ's love for us in turn stimulates our love for Him. This is Paul's point. The thing that motivates him is Christ's love for mankind in general and for him in particular.

In essence, Paul is saying, "I do what I do; I don't do what I don't do; I keep on keeping on; I relentlessly pursue that for which I was called—*because of the love of Christ for me.*" And that motivation should be identifiable in our own hearts and lives as well.

Getting a handle on Christ's love also means getting a handle on the human condition. Two key thoughts the Apostle Paul expresses on this subject are the realities of human sinfulness and human estrangement from God. Paul never apologizes for using the word *sin.* In 2 Corinthians 5:19 he writes, "God was reconciling the world to Himself in Christ, not counting men's sin against them." And in verse 21 of the same chapter he says, "God made Him [Jesus Christ] who had no sin to be sin [a sin offering] for us."

Today we need to recognize anew the true scope of human sinfulness, realizing it is the spiritual dilemma of "bad" people and "good" people alike. We need to be careful not to confuse human sinfulness with sins, for it is wrong to believe that we are sinners because we commit sins. In fact, we commit sins because we are sinners. Everyone is equally a sinner. That doesn't mean that the sins resulting from "sinnerhood" will be the same, of course.

The sins that come out of our sinfulness will be determined by our personality, our environment, and circumstances.

For instance, it is an inescapable fact that if a person is born in poverty, he is much more likely to end up in jail than if he is born to middle- or upper-class parents. It is an inescapable fact that if a person is brought up in a certain type of home, he is much more likely to be attracted to homosexuality than if his family environment were different. But this does not mean that he is a sinner because he engages in homosexual activity or because he steals. He is a sinner *to begin with*, and his innate sinfulness is demonstrated by these sinful behaviors which are determined to a large extent by his background. I cannot stress this point strongly enough. *We are all equally sinful.*

What then is the essence of our sinfulness? It is our independence from God. It is what the Apostle Paul calls elsewhere our "hostility" toward God (Romans 8:7). It is our lack of trust in God, our lack of love for Him. Scripture says that we come from God and we go to God and that our sole reason for being is God. Yet if we human beings ignore, despise, reject, or simply regard as irrelevant the One who created us, then we remove from our humanity the one thing that makes us uniquely human. Such defiance will demonstrate itself in a disregard for God's law, in a distaste for God's holiness, in a disinterest in God's person. It will show itself in 1,001 different ways, but the root problem is human sinfulness. All of us, if we are honest, can identify this disease in our lives.

Paul next discusses human estrangement. It's obvious that one of the powerful themes in 2 Corinthians 5 is that of reconciliation to God. Why do we need to be reconciled to God? For the simple reason that we have become estranged from Him.

The idea of estrangement is not too hard for us to understand. Not infrequently, parents come to me upset that their son or daughter is engaged to be married to someone totally unsuitable. Sometimes, in extreme cases, they will say, "Listen, we are completely opposed to this marriage. And we refuse to have anything to do with it. We're going to boycott the wedding."

Whenever they tell me that, I always strongly advise, "Don't boycott it. Go. Please go." Unfortunately, they usually have already made up their minds by then.

Why do I encourage parents to go to a wedding they oppose? Because when a daughter or son gets married, regardless to whom, there's a very high probability that grandchildren will arrive. When they do, there's a high probability that the grandparents will want to see them and photograph them and brag about them. But if the parents refuse to go to their child's wedding, there's also a very high probability that later he or she will say, "You weren't interested in our wedding. Why are you suddenly interested in the results of it? Forget about seeing the grandchildren!" I've seen it happen over and over again. The grandparents have unintentionally caused a serious family estrangement. And what do they long for more than anything else? Reconciliation!

Now then, if we haven't done something to cause an estrangement, we obviously don't need reconciliation. But if we have done something to cause an estrangement, we're going to have to work like crazy on reconciliation. We can understand that. What we don't understand very often is this: the very nature of our sinfulness has inevitably produced an estrangement from God. And that tragic separation, that loss of meaningful relationship can add up to nothing more than a shallow, self-centered existence and a hopeless eternity. That is the human dilemma.

Having defined our sorry condition, Paul progresses quite naturally into the area of human need. It's very important that we address this issue too.

People today talk about two kinds of needs: *felt needs*, which generate lots of interest, and *real needs*, which are not nearly as apparent. Real needs, however, are the root problems; felt needs are often only the symptoms. I'm sure that if we polled any congregation and asked people to talk about their real needs, several areas of insufficiency would emerge; but if we asked for felt needs, the responses would be far greater.

Let me illustrate. After I preached a series of messages on the fruit of the Spirit some time ago, a lady came up to me and inquired, "When are you going to preach about something that really matters around here? Our families are falling apart. When are you going to tell us how to put our families back together again?"

So I asked in return, "Do you have problems in your family?"

"Yes."

"Well, would a little love help?"

"It sure would."

"Do you think patience would help?"

"It certainly would."

"How about a little bit of long-suffering, faithfulness, gentleness, and meekness?"

"Those are exactly what we need."

I was trying to get her to see that I had just given a series on love, joy, peace, patience, gentleness, meekness, self-control—all the things that would put families together again. She was thinking *family*, a felt need; she wasn't understanding her real need, which was to have the Spirit of God work in the lives of her family members to bring healing.

Our felt needs can show up all over the place. Our real needs can be put in a universal nutshell: first, the need to restore our relationship with God—reconciliation; and, second, the need to have our sin dealt with—justification. Only when these real needs are met can our felt needs be truly satisfied.

And that is the great hope offered in this passage of Scripture, for here Paul makes clear the possibility that estranged people *can* be reconciled to God and sinful people *can* be justified by God. By reconciliation, he means that men and women who have gone far away from God can be brought back to Him and restored to the relationship that they ought to have. By justification, among other things he means that we can have our sins totally forgiven. Not only that, we can even have the righteousness of Christ credited to our account. That's what Paul says in 2 Corinthians 5:21: "God made Him [Christ] who had no sin to be sin for us, so that in Him we might become the righteousness of God."

Next Paul talks about divine initiative. Let's accept the fact of our sinful human condition. Let's accept the fact of our deep human need. The big question is how do we get these needs met and solve our sin problem? How do we meet our need for justification?

Some people might advise us to get religious. Others might suggest we attend some seminars. Still others might tell us to get our act together or exhort us to try our hardest and hope that everything works out in the end. But none of these "solutions" provides the answer. What's more, the initiative to deal with these problems and meet these needs does not rest with mankind at all. It rests entirely with God.

One of the healthiest things a human being can ever do is, having understood what he can do, to then understand what he can't do. Each of us must eventually come to realize that we cannot make ourselves right with God, no matter what initiatives we take. However, the glorious news of the Gospel is that God, who must take the initiative if anything is to happen, *has* taken that initiative.

He sent His only Son, Jesus Christ, to die for our sins. Because of the Cross of Calvary, reconciliation has been made possible, and man can be made right with God.

Some of us never grasp this truth because we have an erroneous view of God. We see Him as sort of a celestial teddy bear or grandfather—neat, kind of cute, perhaps slightly absentminded. But the Bible teaches that God is the God of righteousness and holiness as well as the God of love and grace. The idea that He is warm and fuzzy, loving and forgetful is comforting, especially if we don't want to think seriously about our sin. If that manmade fabrication were so, we might reason God responding to us: "No, naughty, you shouldn't have done that. But don't worry. No sweat. Just wash up and forget about it." However, such a Sovereign of the universe would hardly be just or holy, and would most certainly not be righteous.

God's very nature requires judgment for sin. And the judgment for sin is death—*our* deaths. But the Lord Jesus, our spotless, sinless substitute, came to earth, bore our sin, accepted our judgment, and died *for* us. The initiative was all God's.

Now we can be reconciled to God. Now we can be forgiven our sins. Now the depths of our real needs can be satisfied. God has maintained His integrity. He has fully demonstrated His love, and at the same time dealt in all holiness and righteousness with sin. Now He is perfectly free to forgive and to have men, women, and children reconciled to Himself. The emphasis, however, must always be on the divine initiative.

And so comes Paul's appeal—"We implore you on Christ's behalf: be reconciled to God" (2 Corinthians 5:20). Of course, many people in the 1st century as well as the 20th act as if God should be reconciled to them. They live life as if to say, "I'm here and God's out there, and if God and I are to get along, He needs to come to me. He needs to see things my way and endorse what I've decided." That's not biblical. God stands at the Cross and through His servants, His ambassadors, He appeals to people, "Oh, please listen. Reconciliation is available. Forgiveness is available. Justification is available. You can be made right with Me. All you have to do is respond to My appeal and do it My way. Please come!"

Faced with this solution, we need to ask: what was the divine motivation? Why would God do this? It was not our love for God that initiated the Cross. It was not our worthiness or perfection. It started utterly and completely in the heart and mind and character of God. It was the grace of

God and the love of Christ that motivated the sacrifice at Calvary. No Cross, no reconciliation. No death of Christ, no forgiveness. No grace of God, no possibility of estranged people being restored to Him. But because there was grace, because there was love, there was the Cross. And because there was the Cross, there is reconciliation and justification.

But in case I doubt, how do I know for sure that Christ loves *me?* First, because He was prepared to die for me and did indeed suffer the pain of crucifixion. Second, because He was willing, even though He was sinless, to be made sin for me. That's how I know He loves me.

It is this love of Christ that Paul maintains is his primary motivation in life, but how does he get from a point of theology to the daily application of it? How do we get from the point of believing all about justification, reconciliation, substitution, and other big words to stepping out and laying our bodies on the line?

A very important word in 2 Corinthians 5:14 will help us here: "For Christ's love compels us, because we are *convinced*" (italics added). In other words, the Apostle Paul has taken all this information, thought it through, and arrived at a conclusion that is relentlessly logical. The key to his motivation is that he understands the love of Christ demonstrated at the Cross, and because of it there has been born within him an undying conviction. That's what he means when he writes, "Christ's love compels us, because we are convinced that One died for all, and therefore all died. And He died for all, that those who live should no longer live for themselves but for Him who died for them and was raised again" (2 Corinthians 5:14-15).

"One died for all, and therefore all died." What on earth does that mean? Well, first of all, it means that when we say Christ died for sin, we identify with Christ's death on our behalf and God views us just as if we truly did die. If the wages of sin is death, if Christ died for our sins, and God looks upon us as if we died with Christ, then the wages for our sin have been paid. The punishment for our sin has already been meted out. We have already been judged in Christ, and if that is true, Paul says we need no longer fear condemnation (Romans 8:1).

But there's another aspect to this phrase. When Christ died, He died for sins. Can you imagine believing this to be so, yet continuing to embrace that for which Christ died? Here's a horrendous sin in my life and I say to myself, "Christ loved me enough to have died for that sin, but I'm going to continue to do it anyway." If I believe this sin was so heinous in God's sight that it necessitated the death of Christ, yet I continue in it, I love what God hates. Is that consistent? Obviously not.

So Paul arrives at another conclusion: believers die *to* what Christ died *for*.

If it was your adultery that necessitated Christ's death on the cross, don't say, "Forgive me, Jesus," and go on committing adultery. If it was your hatred and bitterness that necessitated Christ's death on the cross, recognize that if He died for you, you died in Him and died to that hatred and bitterness as well.

To clarify this conviction, Paul gives a beautiful picture: "If anyone is in Christ, he is a new creation; the old has gone, the new has come" (2 Corinthians 5:17). Those for whom Christ has died, those who have died in Christ, recognize they no longer live for themselves. Instead, they live for Him. There's no newer perspective than for a person to stop living for himself and to start living for Christ. There's nothing more radical, nothing more likely to change a person than for him to say, "I've died to my old life of selfishness and independence from God. I'm through with it. I now choose to live for Him who died for me and rose again. The old has gone. The new has come. I am a new creation in Christ Jesus."

This new perspective raises new questions. How can the old pass away? How can the new come? How can we be new creations in Christ? Paul says, "Because of the love of Christ." There is absolutely no other way. If anything of significance has ever transpired in my life, it is attributable to the grace of God channeled through the love of Christ, manifested in His death and resurrection on my behalf. The love of Christ compels me.

RESPONDING TO THE LOVE OF CHRIST

Now then, it's one thing to understand all this, but quite another to respond to it. So I want to go back to the verb *compel* at the beginning of 2 Corinthians 5:14. What does the word mean and what are we compelled to do?

The word translated *compel* here is the Greek verb *sunecho*, which is used several times throughout the New Testament. For example, when the Lord Jesus was arrested in Gethsemane, He had a soldier on one hand and a soldier on the other. As these two men held onto Christ, the word used to describe what they were doing is *sunecho*. They were compelling Him, or, better yet, constraining Him. In another instance, when Stephen preached before the Sanhedrin prior to being stoned to death, the people didn't want to hear what he had to say, so they covered their ears. One hand on one ear, one hand on the other. The word used to describe their action is *sunecho*. A third instance is from Paul's own life and his confession, "For to me, to live is Christ and to die is gain" (Philippians 1:21). In essence, he goes on to say, "I don't know which I'd choose, assuming I even could. I'd love to die and be with Christ. On the other hand, I'd love to live and be able to minister to you. I'm torn between the two." In the *King James Version*, Philippians 1:23 is translated this way: "I am in a strait betwixt two." *Sunecho* is the word. It's as if a person had two walls locking him in, keeping him on track, keeping him on "the straight and narrow." That's the idea of *compel* in this passage.

The Apostle Paul understands the love of Christ. He also understands what Christ has done in his life and is totally locked in by it. He says in effect, "I feel the love of Christ so powerfully that when I want to drift off this way, it locks me in; and when I want to wander off the other way, it locks me in. I can't get away from the love of Christ. It constrains me, compels me, keeps me on track."

Why is it that so many Christians get off track? Why is it that so many Christians wander away from the faith? The answer is very simple. The love of Christ is not operative in their lives. They have lost sight of it and it is no longer locking them in—but something else is. What do we love more than Christ? What is it that motivates us more?

The Bible talks about the love of money. That'll do it. Or the love of man, too great a concern for what people think about us. Scripture warns of all kinds of things that can take the Lord's rightful place in our lives. When that happens, it's the easiest thing in the world to drift away. But when the love of Christ is our central focus, He'll keep us on track.

Once we truly understand the love of Christ, we feel an overwhelming compulsion to love the One without whose love we would be lost. Indeed, one of the delightful things about being loved is finding within your heart a desire to love that person back.

A personal example of this will illustrate how this is so. As my wife and I spent time together one recent weekend, she told me on a number of occasions that she loved me. It was something that she wanted to tell me. In other words, it was of her own free will. The interesting thing was how I responded to that verbal affection. The more she told me she loved me, the more I wanted to tell her how much I appreciated her love, how it encouraged and affirmed me— and together we discovered that we were able to respond to each other in a deeper way. It's a natural thing. When I understand the love of Jill, the love for Jill is something that comes welling out of my heart, and vice versa. When I understand the love of Christ for me, something is strangely wrong if a love for Christ does not result.

Once I grasp and begin to respond to Christ's love, once I really love the Christ whose love for me made all the difference, than I also begin to love those who, without Christ's love, are as lost as I was before I discovered it. What a strange thing it would be if I were to say, "I am moved by the love of Christ that took Him to the cross to die for all people," yet I had no love whatsoever for those who have never been reconciled and justified. Christian motivation, based on the love of Christ, should begin to stimulate in me love for Christ, but then it should go further and stimulate in me a love for unbelievers who need the Saviour.

"Paul, why did you keep on doing what you were doing?"

"For the love of Christ."

"Why did you go to all those faraway places?"

"For the love of Christ."

"Why did you bother with all those nasty people?"

"For the love of Christ"

"Aw, come on, Paul. What's the big deal about the love of Christ?"

"You don't know? Do you know where I was without the love of Christ? Do you know what would have happened to me without the love of Christ? More importantly, do you know where *you* are without the love of Christ? Do you know where you will be throughout eternity without the love of Christ?"

Paul would come back loud and clear on all these points. You'd begin to say, "I understand that guy. I understand what's happening to him. He is locked in by the love of Christ."

REFLECTING THE LOVE OF CHRIST

How does all this work *for us?* How do we reflect the love of Christ in our lives? The answer: it takes *discerning;* it takes *desiring;* and it takes *deciding.* I find these three words crop up just about everywhere in spiritual experience. Discerning, desiring, and deciding.

If the love of Christ is to become a powerful motivating factor in our lives, we're going to need spiritual discernment in order to understand it, come to a conclusion about it, and arrive at a solid conviction about it. That spiritual discernment will come through the work of the Holy Spirit, taking the Word of God home to our hearts. And it needs to be a regular, constant process.

I firmly believe that Christians need a daily reminder of the love of Christ. I have some very dear friends in Western Europe, friends I made during my years of travel and ministry there. I haven't been back for years, but I still have many vivid memories. One of those memories is that most of those delightful, believing friends had on their desks a cross which bore the form of the crucified Christ. When I asked them about it, they said, "It is impossible for us to go to our desks without being reminded of the Cross of Christ." What they were really saying was this: "It is impossible for us to go through a day without being reminded of the love of Christ." While the case for Christian symbolism is perhaps debatable, I use this example as a reminder that we all need to constantly remember the love of Christ. Whatever it takes to remind us on a regular basis, let's do it, for we need ongoing discernment. Where would I be without the love of Christ? Who am I because of the love of Christ?

Then discernment should stimulate a desire within us to know the love of Christ more fully in our lives, to appreciate it more deeply, to respond to it more consistently. Just a caution here: it is possible for us to inadequately discern the love of Christ. If that happens, there will be an insufficient desire to respond properly.

After discerning and desiring comes deciding—the decision that, yes, the love of Christ will be the dominant theme in our lives, that it will motivate all of our choices. We will do the simple things for the love of Christ. We will do big things for the love of Christ. We will not do certain things because the love of Christ took Him to the cross to die for those very things. We might have a hard time giving up some things we shouldn't be doing or starting some things we should be doing. But it's amazing how different our lives will be if, because of the love of Christ, we are now able to decide as we ought; to be, in His power, what He wants us to be; to do through His power what He tells us to do. I can think of nothing more exciting than to be motivated by the love of Christ!

May I encourage you to get a handle on *all* of the motivational factors we've discussed throughout the pages of this book. Different things will motivate you at different times. Some days the love of Christ will do the trick. Some days it will be the gratitude attitude. Sometimes it will be the servant spirit. Sometimes you will need to be hit over the head with a healthy fear of the Lord. Another time you'll just need to be poked or prodded to keep on keeping on. Sometimes you'll be gripped by an overwhelming sense of privilege. It really doesn't matter which of these scriptural dynamics motivates you because all are responses to the initiatives that God has taken in your life. Therein lies the uniqueness of Christian motivation.

PERSONAL REFLECTION

Gracious Father, thank You for Your love manifested in Jesus Christ. Thank You for every opportunity that I have to understand it more fully and appreciate it more deeply. And as I come before You now, I ask that by Your Spirit I might discern these truths more clearly than ever before, that I might have a new sense of desire in my heart no longer to live for myself but for Him who died for me and rose again. May I be able to say on a regular basis, "Yes, it is the love of Christ that compels me!"